STATES UNITED

McCourtney Institute for Democracy

The Pennsylvania State University's McCourtney Institute for Democracy (http://democracyinstitute.la.psu.edu) was founded in 2012 as an interdisciplinary center for research, teaching, and outreach on democracy. The institute coordinates innovative programs and projects in collaboration with the Center for American Political Responsiveness and the Center for Democratic Deliberation.

Laurence and Lynne Brown Democracy Medal

The Laurence and Lynne Brown Democracy Medal recognizes outstanding individuals, groups, and organizations that produce exceptional innovations to further democracy in the United States or around the world. In even numbered years, the medal spotlights practical innovations, such as new institutions, laws, technologies, or movements that advance the cause of democracy. Awards given in odd numbered years highlight advances in democratic theory that enrich philosophical conceptions of democracy or empirical models of democratic behavior, institutions, or systems.

STATES UNITED

A SURVIVAL GUIDE FOR OUR DEMOCRACY

JOANNA LYDGATE, NORMAN EISEN, AND CHRISTINE TODD WHITMAN

CORNELL UNIVERSITY PRESS

Ithaca and London

Thanks to generous funding from the McCourtney Institute for Democracy at Pennsylvania State University, the ebook editions of this book are available as open access volumes through the Cornell Open initiative.

First published 2022 by Cornell University Press

Librarians: A CIP catalog record for this book is available from the Library of Congress.

Library of Congress Control Number: 2022941392

ISBN: 978-1-5017-7007-4 (paperback)
ISBN: 978-1-5017-7008-1 (epub)
ISBN: 978-1-5017-7009-8 (pdf)

Contents

v

Introduction

The attack on the United States Capitol on January 6, 2021, is an enduring symbol of the country's current antidemocracy movement. Images of the assault are burned into national memory. Americans watched as a violent mob scaled walls, overwhelmed law enforcement officers, occupied Congress, and delayed the constitutional certification of a presidential election. This was not a spontaneous protest that got out of hand. It was a coordinated insurrection, fueled by an onslaught of disinformation. January 6 was only the most explosive expression of a campaign against democracy that was instigated much earlier and that continues to this day. Its objectives are to undermine free and fair elections, suppress voting rights, and, ultimately, overturn the will of the voters.

This antidemocracy campaign must be stopped, and we believe it can be. This is the story of how our organization, the States United Democracy Center, has been building a bulwark against it since the summer before the insurrection.

Although there were many earlier indications of a growing movement against democracy, by the middle of 2020, alarming antidemocracy rhetoric became impossible to ignore. The loudest voice belonged to the sitting president, Donald Trump. In July, he proposed delaying the presidential election. In August, he admitted to blocking funding to the United States Postal Service, which would make it harder to process mail-in ballots. By September, antidemocracy forces were continually spreading lies and sowing doubt about the integrity of the upcoming election. Trump was telling white supremacist groups to "stand back and stand by"[1] and instructing his supporters to "go to the polls and watch very carefully."[2] The president and his sympathizers were hard at work undermining the results of an election that had not yet even happened.

At that time, one of us, Joanna Lydgate, was serving as chief deputy attorney general in the Massachusetts Attorney General's Office. In that capacity, she coordinated multistate, bipartisan litigation on issues like the opioid epidemic, consumer protection, data privacy, and financial services. She worked with other states to defend the rule of law and the Constitution during the Trump administration, including successful challenges to the administration's travel ban, family separation policy, and environmental rollbacks. She also oversaw the office's criminal prosecutions, working closely with law enforcement. Joanna understood the power and the responsibility that states have to uphold the law. She recognized both that the states would face unprecedented legal challenges arising from the 2020 presidential election and that state officials critical to that battle would benefit from additional resources. The problem was so urgent that it compelled her to step away from her role as chief deputy to lead an effort to protect the upcoming election.

Norm Eisen had deep experience in both law and politics. He brought expertise in ethics and government reform, having served as special counsel and special assistant to President Barack Obama from 2009 to 2011, and as a US ambassador to the Czech Republic advancing those issues abroad from 2011 to 2014. And as recently as 2019 to 2020, he had served as special counsel to the House Judiciary Committee for the first impeachment and trial of President Trump for abuse of power. Throughout the Trump administration, Norm provided legal services to state attorneys general as they responded to administration actions like those noted above—and during the summer of 2020, those state officials increasingly reached out to Norm for advice and counsel on the gathering threats to democracy, emphasizing the need to provide expert information and legal support to these and other state officials. Together, Norm and Joanna agreed on the pressing need for a state-focused effort to protect the election. They also knew it needed to be both powerful and bipartisan.

Christine Todd Whitman served as governor of New Jersey from 1994 to 2001 and as administrator of the Environmental Protection Agency from 2001 to 2003. In 2005, Governor Whitman published her book, *It's My Party Too: The Battle for the Heart of the GOP and the Future of America*, in which she advocated for the role of moderate Republicans within the party and the need to reestablish a centrist dialogue and fend off the rise of zealous conservatism. As governor, she had interacted with Trump, and as he became more politically active and ultimately won the 2016 election, Governor Whitman grew alarmed by his disrespect for the rule of law. She also understood the danger for the future of our democracy if we lost faith in our public institutions. Beginning in 2018, Governor Whitman cochaired the National Task Force on the Rule of Law and Democracy at the Brennan Center for Justice. After watching the violent rhetoric and the antidemocracy efforts to undermine the 2020 election, she eagerly joined forces with Joanna and Norm to create a bipartisan vehicle to help support democracy.

Recognizing that America could not count on democracy-denying federal and state leaders to defend elections as part of their job description, the three of us started an initiative that has become the States United Democracy Center. Our work is rooted in the premise that state and local officials hold the keys to our democracy. People often think of elections as national events, but they are carried out by the states, according to the rules and policies established by each state.

State and local authorities are responsible for regulating access to the ballot, overseeing the election, counting ballots, certifying results, and protecting those results when they are challenged in court.

Free and fair elections are the foundation of democracy, and they need protection. In this essay, we explain our plan for how to do that. We also explain our two founding principles: any defense of democracy must be bipartisan, and it must be rooted in the states.

The States United Democracy Center

A merican democracy has never been perfect. Despite substantial progress, our country's founding documents contain aspirational goals of equality and justice that have yet to be fully realized more than two centuries later. The United States has struggled at times throughout its history to reach its democratic potential, but the threat today is the gravest in decades.

One troubling indicator is that Americans are intensely divided and often rely on entirely different perceived facts as bases for entrenched positions. Another is that polling shows that an increasing number of Americans believe that "true American patriots might have to resort to violence in order to save our country."[3] In 2021, the United States was classified as a "backsliding" democracy by the International Institute for Democracy and Electoral Assistance's annual report on the Global State of Democracy.[4] In its report, the institute said that the United States, "the bastion of global democracy, fell victim to authoritarian tendencies itself, and was knocked down a significant number of steps on the democratic scale."[5]

Although Americans like to think that their own democracy is uniquely protected, no democracy is immune from challenge, and no democracy can be taken for granted. Throughout history, we see examples of democracies that failed, or that survived only through struggle and great sacrifice. As we write, the people of Ukraine are fighting and dying for some of the very privileges that are under pressure across states in our country.

In America, the coming years will be critical when it comes to countering the troubling indicators above. If antidemocracy candidates win important state and local positions in the 2022 midterm elections, they will be in much stronger positions to exert pressure on the 2024 presidential election. Despite the very real threat, our experience gives us hope that together we can win this fight against the antidemocracy forces and protect our free and fair elections. Our work demands support for and protection of state and local officials, a strong countering of election lies and misinformation, and accountability for those who step outside the bounds of our democracy. It also requires Americans to help by paying attention, seeking out true information, and engaging in their state and local elections. This is difficult work, but we believe there is cause for optimism.

Our Approach: State-Focused and Bipartisan

Two principles define the States United Democracy Center. First, our primary focus is on the state and local levels of government across the United States. The states are where democracy is under attack, and the states are where democracy must be defended. We are the only election-protection organization that was founded to provide direct legal, research, and communications support to those officials who are on the front lines of protecting our democracy. As we discuss in more detail below, we direct our bipartisan, state-focused efforts in four specific areas: (1) election protection, (2) political violence prevention, (3) accountability, and (4) truth in elections.

Second, bipartisanship is in our DNA. We recognize that the list of state and local officials who stood firm in defending democracy during the 2020 election includes Democrats and Republicans alike. We believe strongly that an explicitly bipartisan approach is the only lasting way to defend democracy. At States United, we work with state officials, including law enforcement leaders, in a bipartisan manner. We provide support and information to any state officials interested in protecting the integrity of their elections, and we applaud the efforts of any state officials who stand up against the antidemocracy forces attacking the integrity of their elections. We also understand the particular value of Republican leaders voicing confidence in the legitimacy of our elections and the power those voices have to influence a wide range of American voters.

Our Challenge: The Antidemocracy Threat

Since January 6, Republican-led state legislatures, fueled by conspiracy theories, unfounded assertions, and blatant lies, have demanded new audits of already certified, litigated, and officially audited election results. They have also passed bills designed to make voting more difficult in a myriad of ways. The antidemocracy movement has learned from its failure to overturn the 2020 presidential election, and many of the same people who spread lies and advocated violence to change its valid results have developed a playbook to control election outcomes in the future.

Just like ours, their playbook recognizes that the battle is being waged on the state level. First, antidemocracy forces are working to pass laws granting the state legislature increased control over "practically every step of the electoral process."[6] These bills aim to make highly partisan Republican state legislatures the final arbiter of election results, grant them power to micromanage election administration, limit local election officials' ability to administer elections effectively, threaten those officials with potential fines and criminal charges, and seize power to fill those ostensibly nonpartisan election positions. Second, the antidemocracy movement is sponsoring candidates for state and local election positions who continue to undermine or outright deny the valid results of the last presidential election.

Through these efforts to *change the rules* and *change the referees*, the antidemocracy movement is setting itself up to *change the results*—that is, to override any outcome in which its preferred candidate does not win. These efforts constitute a full-fledged attack on our democracy.

Our Origins: Protecting the 2020 Election in the States

We organized ourselves in the summer of 2020 and initially called our initiative the Voter Protection Program. What we did over the next few months would test the thesis that defending elections in individual states was the surest way to preserve democracy for the whole country. We worked hand in hand with officials in some of the most closely contested states, and we organized law enforcement leaders to protect elections. We also supported litigation to protect the United States Postal Service, provided voter protection toolkits to attorneys general and police chiefs across the country, brought in election and constitutional experts to provide clear advice to the states, and ensured that strong voices—of both Democrats and Republicans—were making the prodemocracy case in the media and providing accurate election information every day.

The threats to democracy we encountered in the post-election period in 2020 were just the beginning, and they would teach us valuable lessons. Foremost, it was clear after the January 6 insurrection that our work was far from over. The antidemocracy forces began to regroup, gathering steam to continue their efforts. In March 2021, our project evolved into the States United Democracy Center, a 501(c)(3) non-profit, and States United Action, a 501(c)(4) nonprofit, continuing with a distinguished advisory board of former state and federal leaders from both sides of the aisle. Our goal remains the same: to advance free, fair, and secure elections. Our mission is to connect state officials, law enforcement leaders, and prodemocracy partners across America with the tools and expertise they need to safeguard our democracy. We also leverage a pro bono network of many of the most prestigious law firms across the country to help us with this work. We will describe each of these antidemocracy efforts below. And then we will turn our focus to how the battle for democracy is being waged today.

The Movement against Democracy

The current antidemocracy movement in the United States is pushing to its supporters the premise, "If our candidate didn't win, then the election must have been stolen." To be valid, that stance requires evidence of widespread, coordinated fraud, and no such evidence exists. Indeed, all the evidence is to the contrary. So the movement has instead developed a playbook, executed at the state level, to guarantee the election results that it wants. First, as we introduced above, they want to *change the rules* under which elections are run. Second, they want to *change the referees* who apply those laws to administer, oversee, certify, and defend elections. Those two steps then create the pathway to *change the results* of an election.

Long before the current playbook took form, however, antidemocracy forces sought to undermine public confidence in the electoral process. To do that, they worked to plant the idea that something was deeply wrong with American elections. Allegations of "voter fraud," a term that has come to include all manner of election irregularities, have bubbled beneath the surface of discourse about US elections for decades. By 2007, in a report titled "The Truth about Voter Fraud," the Brennan Center for Justice at New York University School of Law noted that it was "easy to find opinion pieces and legislative statements claiming that voter fraud is a substantial concern."[7] The report made note of allegations published by a controversial and short-lived organization called the American Center for Voting Rights, as well as a book, *Stealing Elections*, published by a former member of the *Wall Street Journal*'s editorial board.[8] Aside from a "trickle of news stories of low-grade fraud in a few isolated elections," however, the Brennan Center found that there were few sources documenting specific cases, and its report concluded that substantiated cases of fraud were extraordinarily rare.[9]

Despite those facts, claims of voter fraud endured and gathered strength. Former president Trump's false allegations of election fraud can be traced at least back to 2012. Following President Barack Obama's reelection victory over Mitt Romney, Trump tweeted that the election was a "total sham," and claimed that the United States did not have a democracy.[10] Trump also warned voters to make sure voting machines were not switching their Romney votes to Obama.[11] Two years later, during the November 2014 midterm elections, Trump furthered his conspiracy theory, tweeting, "Crazy - Election officials saying that there is nothing stopping illegal immigrants from voting. This is very bad (unfair) for Republicans!"[12]

Two years after that, Trump himself was the Republican nominee for president. In the closing weeks of the 2016 campaign, as polls showed him trailing Hillary Rodham Clinton, the Democratic nominee, in battleground states, Trump furiously sought to sow doubt about the election to come. In mid-October, he tweeted that the "election is absolutely being rigged by the dishonest and distorted media pushing Crooked Hillary—but also at many polling places—SAD."[13] At the third and final presidential debate, Trump refused to say that he would accept the outcome of the election should he lose to Clinton. Even after he defeated Clinton in the Electoral College to become president-elect, Trump pushed the lie that he had won the popular vote, despite the fact that Clinton had received almost three million more votes.[14]

Trump and his allies pushed conspiracy theories and blatant lies to support their claims of voter fraud. They did so preemptively, aiming to delegitimize any undesirable outcome even before the elections took place.[15] These claims undermined legitimate election results and fomented suspicion among the American public that voting is rigged. They created a baseline of general distrust in democratic institutions, from the government itself to the press, spurred by

Trump's "fake news" campaign.[16] Ultimately, they laid a foundation for an outright assault on democracy waged during the 2020 election and beyond.

The Run-Up to the 2020 Election: Preemptive Attacks and Our Response

During former president Trump's 2020 reelection campaign, he and his allies built on his longstanding efforts to cast doubt on the legitimacy of the voting process. These efforts culminated in a full-scale attempt to overthrow the 2020 presidential election, commonly known as the Stop the Steal movement.

The Stop the Steal movement grew from the baseless theory that expanded mail-in voting, offered in many states because of the COVID-19 pandemic, would allow for rampant voter fraud. Despite a lack of any evidence to that effect, Trump and his allies created this narrative leading up to the 2020 election because of the widely held belief that mail-in ballots would skew heavily toward Joe Biden, the Democratic nominee and former vice president, whose supporters were more likely to follow COVID-19 safety recommendations.[17,18] Trump and his allies attempted to change the results of a legitimate election by working to delay the mail, limit opportunities for mail-in voting, and stop counting ballots after Election Day.

As ever, Trump expounded his conspiracy theories on Twitter. On May 24, he wrote that people were grabbing ballots out of mailboxes and printing "thousands of forgeries."[19] On June 22, he wrote that "MILLIONS OF MAIL-IN BALLOTS" would be printed by foreign countries.[20] On July 30, he increased the false election fraud rhetoric even further, tweeting, "2020 will be the most INACCURATE & FRAUDULENT Election in history. . . . Delay the Election until people can properly, securely and safely vote???"[21]

Trump also refused to guarantee a peaceful transition of power should he lose. For example, when asked on July 19 in a *Fox News Sunday* interview whether he would commit to accepting the election results, Trump responded, "I have to see. . . . No, I'm not going to just say yes. I'm not going to say no, and I didn't last time, either."[22] In fact, Trump was unwilling to acknowledge the possibility that he could lose, pushing the premise that if he were to lose, the election would, by definition, have been fraudulent. On August 20, he said, "So this is just a way they're trying to steal the election, and everybody knows that. Because the only way they're going to win is by a rigged election."[23] Well before any votes were cast in 2020, Trump established a pattern of delegitimizing an election that polls repeatedly showed him poised to lose.

It was during this summer of foreboding for our democracy that we formed the Voter Protection Program (VPP). Our mission was to provide support to the states on the front lines of defending our elections. From the start, we worked in states where the vote was being challenged, advising state officials, initiating and defending against litigation, informing the public about the election process, and fending off voter suppression and misinformation. We were part of a constellation of national, state, and local nonprofit organizations that came together to protect democracy. Our unique contribution was our perspectives as former federal and state officials. By also bringing together a bipartisan coalition of current and former governors, secretaries of state, attorneys general, and law enforcement leaders for the first time, States United—then under the name VPP—helped build a nonpartisan firewall against those trying to undermine democracy in the states.

After Election Day 2020: Attempts to Reverse the Will of the Voters

Between the election on November 3, 2020, and the Electoral College vote certification on January 6, 2021, the Stop the Steal movement explored a variety of ways to overturn the will of the American people. Biden had defeated Trump decisively, both in the popular vote and in the Electoral College, but the antidemocracy forces sought to install Trump for a second term. Their strategy consisted of five interrelated and overlapping tactics, as we describe below. The failure of this strategy delivers an enduring lesson for the defense of democracy. The valid results of an election withstood a methodical attack only because public servants *in the states*, Democrats and Republicans alike, were devoted to the rule of law and fought back.

Tactic 1: Trump-Inspired Protests

As soon as votes were cast on Election Day in 2020, Trump and other leaders of the Stop the Steal movement incited anger and encouraged followers to protest vote-counting efforts in closely contested states. On Election Night, Trump appeared on television and falsely declared that he had won the election. After listing several states where he claimed to be in the lead or nearly so, the president declared, "We're winning Pennsylvania by a tremendous amount."[24] He continued, "We want all voting to stop. We don't want them to find any ballots at four o'clock in the morning and add them to the list."[25] But under Pennsylvania state law, mail-in ballots could not be tabulated until Election Day. It was therefore understandable that a careful count of all valid votes, including mail-in ballots, would extend beyond Election Day. Later on Election Night, Al Schmidt, a Republican commissioner on the Philadelphia County Board of Elections, responded to the president on Twitter: "Philadelphia will NOT stop counting ALL legitimate votes cast by eligible voters. And we will report and report and report until the last vote is counted."[26]

The following night, House Republican leader Kevin McCarthy spoke on Fox News about supposed fraud in vote-counting facilities around the country. He urged listeners to "not be quiet, do not be silent about this. We cannot allow this to happen before our very eyes."[27] In the days and weeks following Election Day, angry protesters threatened, harassed, and accosted staff at counting facilities in cities across the country, demanding to oversee vote counting and questioning the legitimacy of the voting process. In Pennsylvania, former commissioner Schmidt later described his work as "racing against a disinformation campaign that could potentially disenfranchise voters. . . . It's not about the campaign or about who you want to win. This is never about who wins and who doesn't. But if a campaign is trying to disenfranchise the voters of Philadelphia, you can't not respond to it."[28]

There was nothing suspicious about a longer-than-usual count in these cities. Poll workers had to process hundreds of thousands of mail-in ballots. Rather than relying on facts and applauding the careful work to count every valid vote, protesters were motivated by the disinformation and outrage manufactured by Trump and other leaders alleging that ballots were inappropriately and even illegally being counted past Election Day. While votes were still being counted, Trump's supporters began attending Stop the Steal rallies in various cities to protest Biden's victory.[29] These rallies, many of which were attended by pro-Trump state lawmakers, often produced confrontations between Trump supporters and counterprotesters.[30]

In those uncertain hours after the polls closed, we knew that Americans needed to hear a strong, bipartisan message to counter the disinformation. In a statement signed by members of our advisory board, including former governors, attorneys general, and other officials from both political parties, we stressed that the election would not be over until every legal ballot had been counted. "No matter how long it takes," that statement read, "if our democracy is going to work, we need to respect the will of the people."[31]

We also issued guidance to help members of law enforcement grapple with the protests, spelling out both the First Amendment rights of demonstrators and the laws in place to protect the safety of those who were tabulating the vote.[32] The states pressed on with their counts successfully and safely, validating an early lesson of our work: law enforcement must be brought in as a partner to strengthen our democratic process.

Tactic 2: Baseless Litigation

On November 7, four days after the election, Rudy Giuliani announced the Trump campaign's intention to begin litigation over allegations of voter fraud in Pennsylvania and other states.[33] On November 13, Sidney Powell, a lawyer aligned with the Trump campaign, appeared on the Fox Business Network, proclaiming that there had been massive voter fraud "organized and conducted with the help of Silicon Valley people, the big tech companies, the social media companies and even the media companies."[34] Powell filed lawsuits in Arizona, Georgia, Michigan, and Wisconsin, alleging that manipulated voting machines destroyed ballots and switched votes. Each of these lawsuits was dismissed as baseless.[35] The district court in Michigan presciently observed that the lawsuit there seemed to be "less about achieving the relief Plaintiffs seek . . . and more about the impact of their allegations on People's faith in the democratic process and their trust in our government."[36]

In total, Trump and his allies filed sixty-two lawsuits in state and federal courts between November 4, 2020, and January 6, 2021.[37] They lost all but one, and the single victory did not affect the outcome of any state's election.[38] While some cases failed for jurisdictional issues, such as lack of standing, others were dismissed, by judges appointed by members of both parties, because there was no merit to the allegations of voter fraud.[39] For instance, Kelli Ward, a former Arizona senator and the chair of the Arizona Republican Party, filed a lawsuit seeking to overturn Biden's narrow victory in Arizona. The trial court found "no misconduct, no fraud and no effect on the outcome of the election."[40] The Arizona Supreme Court affirmed, holding that Ward "fail[ed] to present any evidence of 'misconduct,' [or] 'illegal votes' . . . let alone establish any degree of fraud or a sufficient error rate that

21

would undermine the certainty of the election results."[41] In another example, attorney Erick Kaardal filed suit in federal court on December 22, 2020, on behalf of a group of voter alliances seeking to block Vice President Michael Pence from counting the Electoral College votes from several states.[42] The judge found the allegations so baseless that she referred Kaardal to a disciplinary committee.[43] Another federal district court judge in Michigan granted a motion for sanctions against Trump's lawyers who brought an election fraud lawsuit there, concluding that the "lawsuit represent[ed] a historic and profound abuse of judicial process."[44] A Colorado state court judge also granted sanctions against lawyers who brought a putative class action alleging widespread voter fraud in the presidential election, finding the plaintiffs' complaint to be "one enormous conspiracy theory."[45]

Indeed, Trump's claims of widespread election fraud were debunked by officials in his own administration. The administration's own Cybersecurity and Infrastructure Security Agency joined a statement on November 12 calling the election "the most secure in American history."[46] On December 1, Attorney General William Barr reportedly told Trump that the theory of voting machine fraud was "demonstrably crazy."[47] And the same day, Barr announced publicly that the Justice Department had not found any widespread election fraud.[48] The states, forced to defend against this deluge of frivolous lawsuits, were joined by members of the legal community, including lawyers from the Voter Protection Program, who stepped up to provide crucial pro bono help.

Tactic 3: A Pressure Campaign Aimed at State Officials

After losing in court after court, Trump and his allies began pressuring officials in swing states to alter election results in Trump's favor. In Arizona, in the weeks following the election, the Republican chair of the Maricopa County Board of Supervisors, Clint Hickman, received calls from the White House, Rudy Giuliani, and Kelli Ward urging the board to announce that it had discovered voting irregularities. Hickman refused these calls, explaining, "We were in litigation at all these points. . . . Whatever needed to be said, [it] needed to be said in a courtroom in front of a judge or a jury."[49] Similarly, Aaron Van Langevelde, a Republican member of the Michigan Board of State Canvassers, recounted that some political leaders urged the board to withhold certification of Michigan's election results "based on unproven allegations of voter fraud, even though we had no legal authority to do so. . . . We were asked to take power we didn't have. What would have been the cost if we had done so? Constitutional chaos and the loss of our integrity."[50] Van Langevelde refused, and Michigan certified its electoral votes for Biden.

Trump and his closest advisers also directly pressured state legislators. In mid-November 2020, days before Michigan certified its election results, Trump invited members of the Michigan state legislature to come to the White House.[51] Less than a week later, he invited several Pennsylvania lawmakers.[52] Giuliani and attorney Jenna Ellis visited members of several state legislatures on Trump's behalf, including in Arizona, Pennsylvania, and Michigan, to reiterate allegations of voter fraud and to pressure lawmakers to take legislative action to overturn the results.[53] On January 2, 2021, Trump spoke by phone with Brad Raffensperger, the Republican secretary of state of Georgia, and encouraged him to "find" enough votes to reverse Biden's victory there. Trump pressed Raffensperger, asserting that "the ballots are corrupt. And you're going to find that they are . . . and you're not reporting it. That's a criminal—that's a criminal offense." Raffensperger did not give in to this pressure, answering instead: "Well, Mr. President, the challenge that you have is the data you have is wrong."[54]

At our organization, we sought to fortify state officials against this pressure campaign and help the public understand what the law prescribed for certification procedures. In a legal memorandum published ahead of the Michigan Board of State Canvassers' meeting, we stressed that the board's role was strictly ministerial. It was responsible for tallying up the canvasses from across the state and was not permitted to dig around for evidence of irregularities, nor to pursue fantastical allegations of fraud.[55] When the details of Trump's call to Raffensperger were brought to light by the *Washington Post*, we outlined potential criminal implications.[56] The Atlanta-area district attorney later impaneled a special grand jury to investigate.[57]

Tactic 4: Fraudulent Attempts to Replace Valid Presidential Electors

In perhaps the boldest antidemocratic effort to invalidate the results of the 2020 election, Republican state leaders in seven states attempted to override validly appointed presidential electors. In these states, Biden had won the popular vote, and thus his slate of presidential electors—and only his slate of electors—had the legal authority to send a certificate to Congress. On December 14, 2020, as Democratic electors in these seven states met to cast their votes for Joe Biden in accordance with their state's popular vote, Republicans who would have been electors if Trump had won in those states also met. Those would-be Trump electors invalidly declared themselves the rightful electors, and "submitted false Electoral College certificates declaring Trump the winner of the presidential election in Arizona, Georgia, Michigan, New Mexico, Nevada, Pennsylvania and Wisconsin."[58] Trump campaign officials reportedly encouraged and coordinated the fake electors in these seven states.[59]

These false Electoral College certificates were designed to provide Vice President Pence a justification to throw out the valid votes submitted to Congress by the Democratic electors and overturn the election. By law and custom, the vice president plays only a ceremonial role in the electoral process. Under Article II of the Constitution and the Electoral Count Act of 1887, the vice president opens the certificates sent by the states' presidential electors and, after the votes have been counted, announces the outcome, certifying the result of the presidential election.[60]

On January 4, 2021, our organization published a definitive guide to the congressional counting procedure.[61] With extensive legal citation, the guide made clear that there was no basis for recognizing sham Trump electors in states certified for Biden, that the vice president's role was subject to clear limits, and that ratification of Biden's victory was the inevitable, and the only proper, result. "There may be sound and fury on January 6," our guide said, "but it will not change the outcome."

Nevertheless, we now know, Trump legal adviser John Eastman concocted a plan to persuade Pence to ignore his legal obligations and refuse to recognize electoral votes from several states based on a claim that there were "multiple slates of electors" in those states (i.e., the valid electors and the sham electors). In a tweet shortly after midnight on January 6, Trump outlined this antidemocratic approach supported by blatant lies: "Many States want to decertify the mistake they made in certifying incorrect & even fraudulent numbers in a process NOT approved by their State Legislatures (which it must be). Mike can send it back!"[62]

Trump placed immense political pressure on Pence to take part in this scheme, essentially presenting the vice president with a choice between violating the Constitution and being denounced by Trump.[63] Trump's pressure on Pence continued on January 6, as Trump announced to his supporters at the Ellipse that morning: "States want to revote. The states got defrauded. They were given false information. They voted on it. Now they want to recertify. They want it back. All Vice President Pence has to do is send it back to the states to recertify and we become president and you are the happiest people."[64]

The House Select Committee to Investigate the January 6th Attack on the United States Capitol later subpoenaed documents from Eastman. A federal court, reviewing a challenge by Eastman, required him to produce the vast majority of the documents, and found that Eastman and Trump more likely than not had committed a federal crime by attempting to obstruct the work of Congress in counting electoral votes.[65] The court called the scheme "a coup in search of a legal theory."[66]

Vice President Pence ultimately rejected Trump's request, upheld the will of the American people, performed his constitutional duty, and certified Biden's victory. In a February 2022 speech, Pence explained that he had no right to overturn the election. "The presidency belongs to the American people, and the American people alone," he said.[67] Pence reminded his audience, "If we lose faith in the Constitution, we won't just lose elections, we will lose our country."[68]

Tactic 5: A Disinformation and Proviolence Campaign Leading to the Capitol Riot

Parallel to all these antidemocratic efforts ran an unceasing disinformation campaign. The antidemocracy movement was bombarding the American public, and particularly its own supporters, with false or misleading stories about election fraud. Just between Election Day and Biden's inauguration on January 20, 2021, NewsGuard, a service that evaluates the credibility of media sources, identified 166 websites in the United States and Europe that were spreading misinformation about voting, the ballot-counting process, and the results of the election.[69] Disinformation also flourished across social media platforms and partisan media outlets, and was amplified by political figures. The myths included the theories that Democrats used manipulated voting machines or mail-in ballots to change votes from Trump to Biden or to add extra votes for Biden; that undocumented immigrants unlawfully cast a significant number of absentee ballots, presumably heavily skewed toward Biden; and that poll workers manipulated ballots at counting centers when demonstrators were not allowed to oversee the counting process.[70] The purpose of this disinformation campaign was to convince a substantial portion of the American public that if Trump lost any election, it could only be the direct result of election fraud.

Leading up to January 6, the effort to overturn Biden's victory included public rallies in Washington, DC, that spread disinformation about election fraud and referenced violence as a necessary means of overturning the election results. Michael Flynn, the former national security adviser, spoke at a December 12 rally and promised that Trump would remain in office.[71] He likened the assembled protesters to the biblical figures who destroyed the walls of Jericho.[72] Lesser-known figures spoke, too: Amanda Chase, a state senator from Virginia, echoed Trump's claim that Biden "cheated to win" and said that she and many other Americans would "never accept these results."[73] She made drastic claims that Trump should declare martial law to conduct an audit of election results in her state.[74] A Stop the Steal organizer, Ali Alexander,[75] tweeted that he was willing to "give my life for this fight," which the Arizona Republican Party then retweeted with the addition, "He is. Are you?"[76]

These calls for violence multiplied leading up to January 6. At a rally at the Ellipse that morning, Giuliani claimed to be aware of "conclusive proof that in the last 10 percent, 15 percent of the vote counted, the votes were deliberately changed." He exhorted the crowd, "Let's have trial by combat."[77] Trump then told supporters that "we won this election, and we won it by a landslide." He challenged them: "If you don't fight like hell, you're not going to have a country anymore."[78] As it became more evident that Vice President Pence was unlikely to cave to Eastman's strategy to undermine the election, anti-democracy forces resorted to one final strategy—violence to interfere with the Electoral College certification. These lies and calls to violence fueled protesters who proceeded to the Capitol, some chanting, "Victory or death!"[79] The mob breached the Capitol, interrupting the vote certification and forcing an evacuation of members of Congress and the vice president. Only through the heroic efforts of the Capitol Police, the DC Metropolitan Police, and the National Guard was order restored and the vote count resumed.

Following the riot, antidemocracy leaders launched a new disinformation campaign to cast the riot as either a defensible protest by patriots or a so-called false-flag operation by leftists to embarrass Trump. Without any factual basis, antidemocracy leaders were still using every opportunity to spread disinformation to undermine the confidence of the American people in the legitimacy of democratic elections.

Lessons of the 2020 Election

Despite the relentless and evolving efforts of the anti-democratic movement to sow doubt and spread mistrust, the 2020 presidential election was free, fair, and accurate. The antidemocracy movement failed in its attempt to overturn an election, and it failed because public servants, devoted to the rule of law, stood up and defended democracy. States across the country adjusted to the realities of the COVID-19 pandemic and worked to protect safe access to the franchise. Judges dismissed lawsuits that threatened our system of free elections. State and local officials—both Republicans and Democrats—pushed ahead to count every vote, sometimes despite threats against their lives and families. State and local election officials chose to do right, in positions where those choices made all the difference. Their

Figure 1. The US Capitol, January 6, 2021. Brent Stirton/Getty Images News via Getty Images.

courage and commitment to democracy should stand as an example. At the same time, we must recognize how difficult it was for these officials to stand firm, and how close the antidemocracy efforts came to succeeding. This close call should stand as a warning. To protect our democracy, we must protect our elections, which means supporting prodemocracy officials of both parties.

The Antidemocracy Movement Today

The antidemocracy movement that we describe in chapter 2 has flourished, despite the 2020 presidential election results and successful transfer of power. Its leaders still refuse to concede that the American public validly elected President Biden. The so-called Big Lie—that the election was stolen from Trump—now animates the cause. Mostly as a response to this lie, the antidemocracy movement has shifted its playbook to controlling future elections. As we have said, this playbook is focused at the state level. First, it aims to *change the rules* of elections. Second, it aims to *change the referees*, the state and local officials who administer elections. The ultimate goal is the ability to *change the results* of elections.

As it executes that playbook, spreading unfounded allegations and blatant lies about American elections, the antidemocracy faction is undermining public confidence in the democratic process. It is also advancing the proposition that political violence is an acceptable—indeed, sometimes even a necessary—part of a valid election system. This tactic includes both lying about and valorizing the violence on January 6. To support state officials in their defense against the antidemocracy movement's attacks, it is imperative that we understand the movement's methods and goals.

The Antidemocracy Playbook

Changing the Rules

Since the 2020 presidential election, a wave of legislative proposals to revise election laws has swept across the country.[80] One organization, the Voting Rights Lab, identified more than 2,500 election-related bills under consideration by state legislatures in 2022.[81] Many would tighten restrictions on registration and voting and would exert partisan control over how elections are administered. The troubling goal of these state legislative efforts is to collapse our system of checks and balances, and place a thumb on the scale of election outcomes.

Some of these bills seem designed to suppress the vote. In various states, they include provisions that limit the number of ballot drop boxes, tighten identification requirements for absentee voting, reduce the availability of mail-in voting, and even limit the provision of water for people waiting in line to vote.[82] Other bills impose proof-of-citizenship requirements to vote in presidential elections,[83] which could disenfranchise tens of thousands of people who are entitled to vote but lack the required documentation.[84]

Since the 2020 election, state legislative efforts have also expanded beyond voter suppression to a new focus on politicizing, criminalizing, and otherwise interfering with the administration of elections.[85] These efforts threaten to paralyze election administration, delay results or make them difficult to certify, and permit election manipulation by partisan antidemocracy actors. Combined, they ultimately raise the likelihood of an election crisis, and in some cases would allow the legislature to overturn the will of the voters.

Traditionally, each state's executive branch and local election officials have run our voting systems. Each state has developed some form of nonpartisan administration and clear procedures, the preconditions for stable and fair elections. These recent legislative efforts would give state legislators new power to disrupt election administration and the reporting of results, and to tilt the electoral playing field toward their preferred candidates. Had such bills been law in 2020, they would have significantly added to the turmoil that surrounded the election, and they would have raised the alarming prospect that the outcome of the presidential election could have been decided contrary to the people's votes. When the losing party overrides the will of the voters, our system of government collapses.

States United joined two partner organizations, Protect Democracy and LawForward, to publish a report, *A Democracy Crisis in the Making*, that tracks these legislative efforts.[86] The May 2022 edition of this report identified 229 bills, under consideration in thirty-three states, that would interfere in one way or another with election administration.[87] Fifty such bills had already been enacted or adopted in 2021 and 2022.

For example, Georgia's S.B. 202, which was signed into law in March 2021, fundamentally alters the balance of power between the executive and legislative branches.[88] The law replaces the directly elected secretary of state as chair of the State Election Board with a chairperson elected by the legislature. The new law empowers the State Election Board—now chaired by a legislative appointee—to investigate and suspend local election officials. Thus, the bill grants the legislature control of the State Election Board, and then grants that board authority to replace local election officials.

As another example, Kansas's H.B. 2332,[89] which was passed by overriding the governor's veto in May 2021,[90] inserts the legislature into crucial election functions, strips the governor of any authority to modify election laws or procedures, and bars the secretary of state from settling any litigation regarding elections without the consent of a legislative council. As a result, in the event of an emergency, such as a flood that renders polling places inaccessible, the governor will be unable to act quickly to modify election procedures. Likewise, the secretary of state will have no authority to resolve issues in court. Effectively, every lawsuit regarding voting in Kansas—potentially everything from the certification of election results to how voter registration is conducted—will be overseen by a group of partisan legislators.

The May 2022 edition of *A Democracy Crisis in the Making* identified many other ways in which legislators were seeking to interfere with election administration. Six states were considering bills to require a hand count of all ballots in the state, an unprecedented move that would increase errors and delay. A bill introduced in Missouri would allow any single registered voter to request a review that would include a recount of all ballots. An Arizona bill would require election officials to report "voting irregularities." The bill does not define this term, but it would nevertheless subject officials who fail to report irregularities to possible criminal charges.

We see these antidemocratic legislative efforts in states that were closely contested in the last presidential election, including Arizona, Georgia, Michigan, Pennsylvania, and Wisconsin. As we describe in more detail below, laws restricting voting rights or interfering with election administration in any of these states could plausibly affect the whole nation. Even in states without narrow election margins, these legislative efforts illustrate a disturbing trend of antidemocracy forces exploring ways to change the election system to suit their ends. Rather than aiming to improve election administration, transparency, or accuracy, these efforts are premised on lies about fraud and are ultimately aimed at granting partisan legislators the ability to wrest election results out of the hands of voters.

Changing the Referees

As we noted, each state conducts its own election. State-wide positions therefore have vast power over how elections are run. Governors sign or veto laws regulating who has access to the franchise and how elections are administered. Attorneys general defend election laws and results in court. Responsibilities for secretaries of state vary, but in many states they enforce election rules, oversee vote tabulation, and certify results.

As they work to change the rules under which elections are run, antidemocracy operatives are also lining up to oversee voting at all levels of the system, from these statewide positions to precinct-level poll workers. At States United, we use the term *election denier* to include any candidate who has falsely claimed that Donald Trump won the 2020 presidential election, has spread lies about the legitimacy of the election, or has otherwise taken action to undermine the election's integrity. Alarmingly, these election deniers are now seeking control of the election machinery in one state after another.

In 2022, thirty-six states have contests for governor, thirty states and the District of Columbia have contests for attorney general, and twenty-seven states have contests for secretary of state. As of May 4, election deniers were on the ballot in roughly two out of every three races for governor and secretary of state, and roughly half the races for attorney general. Many of these candidates have adopted the lie that the 2020 election was stolen from Trump as a basic campaign position.

Among the most successful of these election deniers is Douglas Mastriano, the Republican nominee for governor of Pennsylvania in 2022, who was filmed passing through breached barricades and police lines at the Capitol during the January 6 attack.[91] Primary voters handed him the nomination three months after the House select committee investigating the insurrection issued Mastriano a subpoena to examine his role in a plan to arrange a slate of sham electors for Trump in 2020.[92] In Michigan, the state Republican Party recently endorsed Matthew DePerno for attorney general and Kristina Karamo for secretary of state. Both have promoted false claims of 2020 election fraud.[93] Trump has involved himself closely in these statewide elections. He has linked his many endorsements to candidates' willingness to claim election fraud in states that he lost. For example, Trump endorsed Mark Finchem for Arizona secretary of state, lauding Finchem's "incredibly powerful stance on the massive Voter Fraud that took place in the 2020 Presidential Election Scam."[94] Finchem was outside the Capitol on January 6 and has identified himself as a member of the far-right Oath Keepers militia group.[95]

As of this writing, election deniers have had a mixed record in the 2022 primaries. Some, like Mastriano in

Pennsylvania, have moved to the brink of election. Others, like David Perdue in the Georgia governor's race and Jody Hice in the Georgia secretary of state's race, have been turned away by primary voters. As we explain later, however, success in any of these races in even one swing state could decide a presidential election.

It is not just statewide roles that are important to election administration. Local offices—such as judges and inspectors of elections—can be just as significant.[96] People in these positions oversee polling locations and safeguard the counting of votes. Although partisan judges or inspectors might only affect a small number of votes per precinct, the cumulative effect could tilt statewide elections, too.[97] Election deniers know this, and they are focusing on these local positions. Last year, in two of Pennsylvania's sixty-seven counties, York and Lancaster, almost a dozen candidates for judge or inspector of elections were election deniers.[98] One election denier, who ran to be judge of elections in his precinct, organized buses traveling to Washington for the Stop the Steal rally on January 6.[99] He was viewed as being so outside the mainstream that a fellow Republican urged the leader of the local Democratic committee to find someone to run against him.[100] He won anyway.[101]

Our findings also illustrate a related, important point: many of the efforts to replace existing officials with election deniers do not involve replacing a Democrat with a Republican. Rather, it is often non-election-denying Republicans who face primary challenges from Republican election deniers.[102] Many Republicans have stood up to election lies and supported the rule of law. The attempted takeover of our election system is not a partisan issue; it is a question of commitment to the rule of law over partisanship and the principle that voters alone should determine the outcomes of elections.

Often in conjunction with advocating for election-denier candidates, antidemocracy leaders are also pushing for the formal censure of Republicans who refuse to embrace the election lies. This effort demonstrates the split within the Republican Party between pro- and antidemocracy factions. At the Georgia Republican Party's 2021 convention, Secretary of State Brad Raffensperger was censured for "dereliction of his constitutional duty," and the censure called for him to "commit [himself] to securing Georgia's elections."[103] In Arizona, the Republican Party censured Cindy McCain, former senator Jeff Flake, and Governor Doug Ducey, all of whom refused to support the effort to overturn the 2020 presidential election.[104] At the national level, the Republican National Committee censured Representatives Liz Cheney and Adam Kinzinger, the only two House Republicans who agreed to join the House select committee investigating the January 6 insurrection.[105] The censure resolution faulted Cheney and Kinzinger for "participating in a Democrat-led persecution of ordinary citizens engaged in legitimate political discourse."[106]

Meanwhile, antidemocracy forces continue to encourage threats and intimidation against nonpartisan election officials committed to protecting election integrity. Threats of violence against election officials, both Democrats and Republicans, have exploded in number. A survey commissioned by the Brennan Center found that "one in three election officials feel unsafe because of their job," and "nearly one in five listed threats to their lives as a job-related concern."[107] Reuters conducted a separate investigation and found "hundreds of incidents of intimidation and harassment of election workers and officials nationwide."[108] According to Reuters, "some of the most severe threats" were those directed at Republican officials in Georgia,[109] including Raffensperger. Threats were also made against Philadelphia's two Democratic city commissioners, Lisa Deeley and Omar Sabir.[110] Philadelphia's third city commissioner, Republican Al Schmidt, also received death threats. They were credible enough that police officers were stationed outside his home, and his family was provided a security detail.[111] The dissemination of lies by election deniers, and the related public shaming of and personal attacks on government officials and election workers, have contributed to greater acceptance of intimidation, threats, and violence as part of the democratic process. Inevitably, intimidation and harassment also drive election workers out of their jobs through resignations and early retirements.[112]

Changing the Results

The antidemocracy movement relies on spreading disinformation and lies, as well as stoking fear, anger, and sometimes violence. Since the 2020 election, this faction has employed these tactics to encourage supporters to *change the rules* of elections and to *change the referees* who oversee and defend elections. The goal is the ability to *change the results*. By this we mean undermining the popular will. After all, there are many ways to control and change the results of an election. Before the fact, antidemocracy forces can restrict access to the polls, make it a hassle to vote absentee or by mail, close polling locations and ensure longer lines at others, harass or threaten election officials into quitting, and seize power over previously nonpartisan election administration. After the fact, those same forces can order sham reviews, perpetually cast doubt on the outcome, create delays that sow chaos and uncertainty, and play havoc with the certification or legal defense of legitimate results.

It is not difficult to imagine any number of scenarios by which this kind of interference could tip the balance of a close presidential election in 2024. For example, take Pennsylvania, one of the most closely contested states in the last election. As of May 4, 2022, thirteen bills were pending in the state legislature to politicize or otherwise interfere with election administration.[113] If he were to win the governor's race, Mastriano, the election denier and Republican primary victor, might sign any of those bills into law. Pennsylvania is also unusual in that the governor directly appoints the secretary of state. A Mastriano-appointed secretary of state might simply refuse to certify the results of the 2024 election. (Mastriano, as a state senator, has also proposed stripping the secretary of state of election powers altogether and giving those powers instead to a commission appointed by the governor and the legislature.[114])

Here's another example. Imagine that an election denier is elected as attorney general of a state that is closely contested in the 2024 presidential election. If an antidemocracy group filed suit to challenge the valid results of an election there, the attorney general might try not to defend the case, or might even support the attempted election sabotage. An election-denying secretary of state could attempt to add onerous voter registration requirements to minimize voter participation, authorize illegitimate audits to justify changing vote totals, or refuse to certify legitimate results. In addition, these state officials have a pulpit from which to undermine confidence in our election system by spreading disinformation.

The antidemocracy movement has laid alarming groundwork for overturning an election, and its ability to do so is a result of its own disinformation campaign. According to Ipsos, around a third of Americans now "believe there was fraudulent voting" in 2020, and a fifth "say they are unsure—meaning under half of respondents unequivocally state[d] there was no, or very little, fraudulent voting in the election."[115] That is consistent with a CNN poll released in September 2021 showing that 36 percent of Americans did not believe President Biden won the election.[116] Thus, the circular logic of the antidemocracy movement is completed: many Americans disbelieve the results of the 2020 election, so the antidemocracy movement argues that it must change election laws and control election administration to restore confidence in the system.

In sum, new laws that remove nonpartisan protections make it harder for prodemocracy officials to protect the integrity of our elections. And if antidemocracy officials gain key statewide offices, they may not be interested in protecting elections in the first place, especially if the results are not to their liking. Thus the antidemocracy movement has mounted an aggressive attack at the state level. We must respond at the state level as well, raising up and building on the widespread, bipartisan support that exists in this country for protecting and strengthening the most fundamental feature of our democracy—free and fair elections.

The States Are the Solution

Historically, the federal government has had some oversight responsibility for elections, perhaps most importantly through the Voting Rights Act of 1965, which aimed to protect minority voters from discriminatory voting practices. Section 5 of the VRA required certain states, counties, and townships with a history of voting discrimination to clear changes to their voting laws ahead of time with either the United States attorney general or a panel of the District Court of the District of Columbia.[117] In 2013, however, the United States Supreme Court effectively struck down the heart of Section 5 of the VRA, freeing the identified states to change their election laws without advance federal approval.[118] In 2021, the Democratic National Committee challenged two Arizona state election rules under Section 2 of the VRA, which prohibits any practice resulting in the denial of the right to vote on account of race or color: first, a ban on third-party ballot collection, and second, a rule invalidating ballots cast in the wrong precincts. The United States Supreme Court upheld both Arizona state rules, holding that neither policy violated Section 2 of the VRA.[119]

Alarmed by the rise of the antidemocracy movement and aware of the erosion of federal protection, Democrats in Congress proposed two bills in 2021. The John Lewis Voting Rights Advancement Act would have restored federal preclearance requirements.[120] The Freedom to Vote Act, a narrower version of a previous bill called the For the People Act, would have set minimum standards for early and mail-in voting and required states to conduct transparent election

Figure 2. Karl A. Racine, attorney general for the District of Columbia, announces a federal lawsuit on December 14, 2021, against the Proud Boys and Oath Keepers for the role they played in planning and carrying out the January 6, 2021, attack on the US Capitol. With him, from left, are States United CEO Joanna Lydgate, Congresswoman Eleanor Holmes Norton, Anti-Defamation League CEO and National Director Jonathan A. Greenblatt, and DC Ward 6 Councilmember Charles Allen. Photo by Ralph Alswang.

audits with clear rules and procedures.[121] Senate Republicans were largely responsible for blocking both bills from passing.

As a result of these setbacks, action by pro- and antidemocracy forces is now focused at the state level. The states are where election policies and procedures are adopted, where voting and voter protection plays out, and where protecting the will of the voters is a hands-on effort. If we want to counter the antidemocracy forces who are working hard to influence future elections, we must likewise focus that effort on the states and provide support and resources to the prodemocracy state officials who are the guardians of our democracy.

At States United, we are closely tracking these attempts to change election rules, referees, and results. We believe strongly in the power of our bipartisan, state-centered approach to counter the active antidemocracy movement, and we have developed a clear plan. As we describe in the next chapter, we direct our democracy protection work across four main areas of focus.

States United's Strategy

Our goals at States United are to build trust in elections and in prodemocracy state leaders, to prevent the undermining of free and fair elections, and to defend the will of the American people. Drawing on a century of collective individual experience, as well as what we learned in the fight for democracy in 2020, we have developed four areas of focus for our organization: (1) helping state leaders protect elections; (2) working with law enforcement to prevent political violence; (3) pursuing accountability for those who step outside the bounds of our democracy; and (4) advancing truth and countering disinformation in elections. We believe that success in each of these areas is imperative to protecting American democracy.

Our founding principle of bipartisanship guides our work in each of these four areas. When we bring an ethics complaint as part of our accountability work, for example, we make sure it carries the credibility of well-known signatories from both parties. When we produce guidance for state election officials or law enforcement agencies, it is informed by the practical experience of members of our advisory board, which includes both Republican and Democratic former state officials. And, of course, our public-facing work is meant to inform members of the public in red states and blue states alike. All Americans, regardless of how they vote, have the right to have their votes counted. And all Americans should be warned about disinformation that seeks to spread lies about our elections.

As a national organization operating at a state level, States United provides a platform for state leaders to share information and learn from one another to execute effective election-protection strategies in their own states. We focus our attention where we believe antidemocracy trends pose the greatest threat and where we find prodemocracy leaders who would benefit from our support. While each state faces an array of challenges to voting rights and election integrity, the antidemocracy forces are applying similar tactics across states.

Election Protection

The freedom to vote is the cornerstone of our democracy. It is the freedom that protects all others. As we point out whenever we get the chance, whatever issue you care about most passionately, free and fair elections must come first.

With a focus on the unique tools available to governors, state attorneys general, secretaries of state, and law enforcement, States United develops and promotes nonpartisan legal and policy strategies to protect the vote. We also publish these resources for the public. We offer pro bono legal support to states, counties, and cities from our in-house team of election lawyers and litigators, and from some of the most prestigious law firms in the country—all of us helping defend existing election laws and fight against proposed antidemocracy legislation.

For example, States United served as pro bono co-counsel, alongside Coppersmith Brockelman PLC, for Arizona secretary of state Katie Hobbs as her office defended against a challenge by the Arizona Republican Party.[122] The original lawsuit, filed directly with the Arizona Supreme Court, challenged the state's no-excuse mail-in voting system, which was passed with overwhelming bipartisan support and signed into law by a Republican governor in 1991[123] and which was used by 90 percent of the state's voters in 2020. The suit also challenged Secretary Hobbs's authority to provide drop box and signature verification guidance to county-level election officials under the Arizona Elections Procedures Manual. Hobbs successfully defended against this suit; the court declined to grant jurisdiction, dismissing the case and keeping early voting options intact.[124] The plaintiffs then filed a new lawsuit on

May 17, 2022, in state trial court raising the same claims.[125] On June 6, an Arizona judge rejected those claims, upholding the state's no-excuse mail-in voting system.[126]

In Pennsylvania, States United served as pro bono co-counsel for the Commonwealth in a case brought by Attorney General Josh Shapiro. Shapiro filed suit to block a broad-ranging, state Senate subpoena demanding constitutionally protected personal information about more than nine million registered voters with the intention of handing it over to an unknown third-party vendor.[127] We argued that this subpoena was unlawful, and part of a bad-faith investigation by the State Senate into the 2020 election in Pennsylvania. It threatened to chill future voting—potential voters would rightly fear that the mere act of registering to vote could subject their personal information to disclosure. As States United's legal director, Christine P. Sun, said in announcing the suit, the subpoena was "not a fact-finding mission but rather an attempt to keep the dangerous lies about the 2020 elections alive."[128]

In Texas, States United represents an El Paso County election official in litigation brought by other parties challenging two 2021 laws passed by the Texas legislature. One of the laws makes voter registration procedures more complicated and confusing.[129] The other law puts unreasonable limits on drive-through voting, early in-person voting, mail-in ballots, and assistance for voters with disabilities.[130] In a friend-of-the-court brief filed in March 2022, the El Paso County official, Lisa Wise, explained that under the 2021 laws she may be subject to criminal penalties for routine outreach and communication work that she does to help make sure every eligible voter in Texas can cast a ballot.[131] These are three examples among many.

In addition to legal support, we also conduct research and policy analysis across the states. That is, we do the legwork and the homework to help legislators and local officials understand what will happen if proposed new laws and policies take effect. We also track state and local elections and outline the consequences of litigation and judicial opinions. We aim to compile this information, make it accessible, and suggest best practices. The goal is to equip prodemocracy advocates with the most complete and accurate information about how to protect elections in their states.

With *A Democracy Crisis in the Making*, the report we described in chapter 3, we called attention to maneuvers by partisan state legislatures to seize greater power over elections, all the way to reserving the right to overturn an election result. As we noted in the report's May 2022 update, these attempts are evolving and accelerating. In anticipation of the 2022 midterm elections, States United Action, our 501(c)(4) organization, created Replacing the Refs, a tool to track all election deniers running for major statewide offices. We first released this tool in February 2022, and we are updating it monthly through November.[132] With these two reports, we strive to quantify and sound an alarm about these partisan attempts to *change the rules* and *change the referees*, respectively.

Finally, we recognize the importance of honest communication and the power of public opinion. We understand that our research and policy initiatives are valuable only if we can broadcast the knowledge we collect quickly and clearly. We work to expose antidemocracy efforts in individual states and demonstrate antidemocracy trends, providing accurate information to help state election officials know what they're facing and how to fight back. We also conduct polling and message testing to help them find the best ways to relay reliable information to the voters they serve.

For example, in June 2021, we commissioned a report outlining the many problems with an unprofessional—and now infamous—review of the 2020 election that was then under way in Arizona's Maricopa County.[133] This review was ordered by the Republican-controlled state Senate and carried out by Cyber Ninjas, an unqualified contractor. Our report was written by Trey Grayson, the Republican former secretary of state of Kentucky, and Barry C. Burden, an esteemed professor of political science and the director of the Elections Research Center at the University of Wisconsin. Grayson and Burden faulted the Cyber Ninjas review for a lack of partisan balance, a flawed ballot review process, an unacceptably high level of built-in error, and insufficient security, among other problems. The report was cited repeatedly by news outlets in Arizona and across the country as they covered the sham review.[134]

We have worked to understand the antidemocracy playbook backward and forward, and then to make both state officials and the public aware of these tactics. We know that our prodemocracy message is supported by state officials and citizens across the political aisle, and we understand the importance of using bipartisan voices to grow that support and reinforce the truth that election integrity is not a partisan issue. Together, all of us can defend our democracy—but only if we know what threatens it.

Political Violence Prevention

The January 6 attack on the US Capitol was the culmination of months of threats against voters, election officials, and our democratic institutions. Since January 6, we have seen increasing levels of hate and threats of violence, fueled by lies and antidemocracy conspiracy theories. The best way to keep elections safe—including officials, voters, and the system itself—is to make sure that law enforcement and local election administrators are working together. This partnership *must* be established and strengthened long before the election itself. States United is unique in its focus on this connection.

In 2020, we issued guidance[135] and provided toolkits[136] to local law enforcement officials and other public safety leaders to help them prevent voter intimidation and prepare for mass demonstrations. We worked with our partners at the Institute for Constitutional Advocacy and Protection at Georgetown University Law Center, 21CP Solutions, and the Crime and Justice Institute to develop these tools, to help public safety leaders understand what constitutes voter intimidation and how and why they should speak out against it. We distributed that guidance to police chiefs and state attorneys general across the country. Then we encouraged them (and other law enforcement leaders) to get out in the media every day—on TV, in print, on the radio, in press briefings—to send the clear message that voter intimidation would not be tolerated. States United later received confirmation that at least one violent extremist group posted our guidance to its members and told them not to go to polling places.

State officials across the country have been inundated with threats against themselves and their families. These officials deserve all the help we can give them in determining how to monitor these threats, how and when to respond to them, and when they should call law enforcement for help. Working closely with state officials across different states, we have identified common trends and are working on both short-term solutions and long-term policy responses to keep election officials safe. We facilitate training for law enforcement, develop guidance on emerging dangers, and help connect election officials with the local security support they need.

In response to threats of violence against our election system, we are working to train election officials on personal and digital safety and working with law enforcement organizations to help officers identify extremists in their ranks. In April 2022, in concert with Georgetown Law's Institute for Constitutional Advocacy and Protection,[137] we published guidance to equip law enforcement agencies with a deeper understanding of First Amendment considerations as they work to eliminate extremism among officers and staff.[138] We provided a detailed explanation of the relevant legal tests and helped law enforcement agencies understand that, because of their unique public safety role and responsibilities, they generally have broad discretion—without running afoul of the First Amendment—to take disciplinary action against officers who express bigoted or extremist views.

We are also developing new resources to address voter intimidation. In advance of the 2022 midterm elections, we prepared a report examining the relevant laws governing poll observers.[139] These are members of the public permitted to monitor conduct at polling places, and they are a feature of elections in almost every state. They add a degree of transparency in the electoral process that promotes public confidence in elections. However, in some cases, poll observers have caused major disruptions. For example, during the 2020 election in Michigan, large groups of partisan poll observers crowded polling sites and attempted to enter vote-counting rooms. Our report aims to provide state-by-state legal guidance covering the power, privileges, and limitations of these volunteers. We outline who is eligible to be a poll observer, what poll observers are permitted to do, and what civil and criminal penalties may apply to interfering with the voting process. We make this information available to anyone who asks for it, including statewide election officials, law enforcement professionals, election administrators, and election-protection groups.

Accountability for Antidemocracy Actors

To prevent future attacks, our system must hold people accountable when they violate the fundamental precepts of our democracy. If we do not insist on that accountability now, antidemocracy groups will redouble their efforts in 2022 and 2024.

At States United, we work with our partners in the states to hold violators accountable through advocacy, investigations, and litigation. We work on civil, criminal, and regulatory actions against election-related abuses of power. We also address questions regarding electoral corruption, incitement, and misconduct. Finally, we support legislative investigations, as well as court sanctions and disciplinary proceedings against attorneys who file baseless antidemocracy lawsuits.

We believe any meaningful accountability must include bringing to justice the people who struck at the heart of our democracy on January 6, 2021. In conjunction with the Anti-Defamation League and two private law firms, States United is serving as pro bono counsel to the District of Columbia's attorney general, Karl A. Racine, in his lawsuit against the Proud Boys, Oath Keepers, and other insurrectionists. Attorney General Racine is seeking financial penalties from these far-right militia groups, given their role in planning and carrying out the deadly Capitol attack.[140] This lawsuit is the first effort by a governmental entity anywhere in the United States to hold individuals and organizations responsible in civil court for the violence that day.

Accountability also means demanding full transparency in the investigation into January 6. Until we uncover all the facts about the insurrection, free and fair elections remain at heightened risk. We worked with a bipartisan coalition of former federal, state, and local officials to file a friend-of-the-court brief in November 2021 opposing Trump's attempt to block the release of documents about the insurrection.[141] A federal district judge denied Trump's petition; Trump lost later rounds at a federal appeals court and the Supreme Court.[142] In May 2022, States United submitted a written statement to the House of Representatives' select committee investigating the January 6 attack.[143] The statement, signed by a bipartisan group of former state officials, sought to define the attack as inseparable from the broader antidemocracy movement in the states, before and since. As another critical piece of our accountability work, we have raised concerns and supported ethics complaints against lawyers who abuse their positions as members of the bar and officers of the court.

In October 2021, we filed an ethics complaint against John Eastman, a member of the California Bar, for his role in Trump's attempts to overturn the 2020 election results.[144] The complaint was supported by twenty-five bipartisan signatories, including former federal district court judges and California Supreme Court justices, numerous former Republican officials, leading law professors, and the Bush and Obama White House ethics advisers.[145] The complaint focused on Eastman's role in spreading false claims about election fraud, the memos he drafted that formed the basis for the campaign to pressure Vice President Pence to refuse to certify the valid election results, and the frivolous lawsuit *Texas v. Pennsylvania* in which he represented Trump before the US Supreme Court.[146] In a supplemental letter the following month, States United incorporated newly reported information about Eastman's role in helping Trump pressure Pence, including his conversations with more than three hundred state legislators on January 2, 2021, in which he encouraged them to replace lawfully appointed slates of presidential electors.[147] In March 2022, the State Bar of California announced a formal ethics investigation into Eastman. The bar's announcement thanked States United and other organizations for their prior submissions and noted that they would serve as the starting point for the bar's investigation.[148] States United has since submitted a second supplemental letter, compiling evidence revealed by the House select committee and a federal judge's findings that Eastman and Trump, in their efforts to persuade Pence to reject or delay the count, likely violated federal criminal law.[149] The second letter suggested that, given Eastman's past and ongoing conduct, including recent efforts to "decertify" the 2020 electors in Wisconsin, the bar should consider interim remedies against Eastman to protect the public.[150]

Similarly, in May 2022, we submitted an ethics complaint against Jenna Ellis, a Colorado attorney who worked for Trump and his campaign and assisted in Trump's attempts to overturn the 2020 election results.[151] The complaint asks the Colorado Supreme Court's Office of Attorney Regulation Counsel to investigate whether Ellis violated her professional and ethical obligations as an attorney by spreading falsehoods about the 2020 election, attempting to persuade Pence to refuse to certify valid electoral votes from six states that Biden won, and providing misleading legal advice premised on the false claims that there were two lawfully certified slates of electors in those states. This complaint, as well, was supported by a bipartisan group of respected and experienced legal experts. We believe these bipartisan efforts to hold violators of democracy accountable are a critical piece of educating the public and protecting the will of American voters.

Truth in Elections

Disinformation is at the heart of the threats to our democracy. Conspiracy theories are being used to undermine trust in elections, justify regressive antivoting laws, recruit an army of election deniers for state and local election positions, discourage voting, and incite political violence. The spread of disinformation has made the job of administering elections much more difficult. States United strives to help states fight back.

To counter the onslaught, we recently added a focus on promoting truth in elections. To that end, we will develop an early warning system for dangerous narratives, prepare state officials to respond to them, encourage social media platforms to take down lies, and pursue accountability for people who use disinformation to undermine our democracy.

As we noted earlier, about a third of the American public wrongly believes that voter fraud determined the outcome of the 2020 election. This myth is sustained and spread by disinformation. One recent example is the coordinated disinformation campaign behind a conspiracy-filled film called *2000 Mules*, which seeks to fuel suspicions about the use of ballot drop boxes.[152] The film has been thoroughly discredited by independent fact-checkers but nevertheless is being used by Trump and others as supposed evidence of fraud that altered the outcome of the 2020 election.[153] An extensive network of bad actors—many seeking fame or profit—is promoting the film. An unfortunate number of people will hear these lies and believe them.

Most concerning is the danger that disinformation will lead to violence. People who believe the 2020 election was stolen from Trump have resorted to threatening election officials and their families. The attack on the Capitol on January 6 was a direct result of a disinformation campaign waged by Trump and his allies. So States United, alongside researchers and analysts, is working on an early warning system to detect the lies that voters are seeing in their states, and then determine which inoculations and countermessages are most effective in fighting them. We are also working to train and brief our state and local partners for this increasingly important part of their jobs.

We face a dangerous asymmetry of election-related information in our media landscape. Online, bad information overwhelms the good. While some are lost down rabbit holes of lies and conspiracy theories, most Americans are seeking the truth about our elections and not always finding it. We and our partners can help by increasing the volume and availability of high-quality, factual information online while we seek to reduce the spread of lies and expose the people and motives behind them. Our four areas of focus are tools aimed at the same goal: supporting prodemocracy state actors in their critical roles as protectors of our American democracy.

GOVERNOR DOUGLAS A. DUCEY

STATE OF ARIZONA
★
PROCLAMATION

CERTIFICATE OF ASCERTAINMENT FOR PRESIDENTIAL ELECTORS

I, Douglas A. Ducey, Governor of the State of Arizona, do hereby certify that:

The Official Canvass of the General Election held on Tuesday, November 3, 2020, shows the following results for the office of Presidential Electors for President and Vice President of the United States, as certified by the boards of supervisors of the several counties of the state of Arizona. The Official Canvass indicates that the following group of eleven individuals:

DEMOCRATIC PARTY PRESIDENTIAL ELECTORS
Presidential Candidate Joseph Biden
Vice Presidential Candidate Kamala Harris

NAME	NUMBER OF VOTES
Gallardo, Steve	1,672,143
Heredia, Luis Alberto	1,672,143
Jackson, Constance	1,672,143
Kennedy, Sandra D.	1,672,143
Lewis, Stephen Roe	1,672,143
McLaughlin, James	1,672,143
Nez, Jonathan	1,672,143
Norris, Ned	1,672,143
Romero, Regina	1,672,143
Rotellini, Felecia	1,672,143
Yamashita, Fred	1,672,143

received the highest number of votes cast for any candidate for this office, and having complied with all provisions required by law for candidates in general elections, they are duly elected Presidential Electors.

I further certify that the following Presidential Electors received the number of votes indicated:

Arizona Certificate of Ascertainment - Page 1

Figure 3.   The first page of Arizona's certificate of ascertainment for presidential electors for the 2020 election, certifying a win for the Biden-Harris ticket. National Archives.

GOVERNOR DOUGLAS A. DUCEY

STATE OF ARIZONA
★
PROCLAMATION

Certificate of Final Determination of Presidential Electors

I, Douglas A. Ducey, Governor of the State of Arizona, pursuant to 3 U.S.C. § 6, hereby certify that the Supreme Court of Arizona made a final determination of an untimely filed controversy or contest concerning the appointment of Arizona's electors in *Burk v. Ducey*, No. CV-20-0349-AP/EL on January 5, 2021. This case upheld the list of electors that was previously certified and filed with the Archivist.

This action completes all outstanding legal action in Arizona's state courts regarding electors for which I am aware. A true and correct copy of the Court's opinion is attached.

IN WITNESS WHEREOF, I have hereunto set my hand and caused to be affixed the Great Seal of the State of Arizona.

GOVERNOR

DONE at the Capitol in Phoenix on this 6th day of January in the year Two Thousand Twenty-One and of the independence of the United States of America the Two Hundred Forty-Fifth.

ATTEST:

Secretary of State

Figure 4.   Arizona Governor Doug Ducey and Secretary of State Katie Hobbs certify the state's final determination of presidential electors after the resolution of legal action. National Archives.

Our System Can Prevail

As the story of this book makes clear, there are good reasons to be concerned for the future of our democracy. But in our work we have also been heartened by the ample reasons for optimism. We outline below some lessons of the fight to protect our elections in 2020 and beyond. We have faith that the virtues of our system will prevail if good people work together to protect our democratic principles.

The 2020 Election Was a Success

Americans who value democracy and want to protect it should take heart in the outcome of the 2020 election. Despite the persistent and disturbing antidemocracy efforts that we have described above, the election succeeded because of tireless work by state and local officials from both political parties who did their jobs, adapted to difficult circumstances, and protected our democracy. The election brought to light not only efforts to undermine free and fair elections, but also the strength of our system and of those officials. They responded nimbly to the constantly changing circumstances of the COVID-19 pandemic. Secretaries of state rolled out sweeping new programs to make voting safe and accessible, governors supported those efforts, and state attorneys general defended them in court. The work of these officials deserves substantial credit for high voter turnout despite the pandemic. Following the 2020 election, these same state officials resisted a tremendous pressure campaign from the defeated candidate. They counted votes carefully, certified accurate results that reflected the will of the voters, and defended those counts and certifications against legal challenges and disinformation campaigns. The many layers of our election system ultimately worked as intended because the individuals responsible for upholding election integrity were committed to respecting the process of democracy above any particular result. Election heroes across the states saved our democracy in 2020, and we were pleased to be among the many who supported their efforts.

These same state and local officials continue to play a critical role in defending democracy. Amplifying their voices is an important part of the ongoing fight. Their expertise and integrity have earned them the trust of voters. At the time of this writing, voters in some states were already demonstrating that trust by rejecting primary challenges from antidemocracy candidates in the spring of 2022. In other places, election deniers may well succeed in November and infiltrate the system. That possibility only underscores the need for voters, journalists, and other stakeholders to draw sharp distinctions between the candidates who seek to protect the democratic process and those who would undermine it. Putting trustworthy officials front and center in our national discourse is a critical piece of providing accurate election information and building confidence in the integrity of the system.

Our responsibility to that system must go beyond the next election. The deep institutional knowledge of state and local election administrators is a bulwark against antidemocracy forces. We must better fund these state offices and protect experienced administrators from harassment and burnout. We must also recruit and train qualified public servants to protect our elections in the future.

Democracy Is a Team Sport

Our efforts to preserve democracy will be stronger and more successful if we all work together. First, prodemocracy state and local officials can learn from and support each other. At States United, we remain focused on helping individual states as well as helping states help each other. We provide platforms for information sharing, for example, to help states identify common problems and find the best solutions.

Second, bipartisanship is key. As the founders of States United, each of us has a commitment to bipartisanship that started well before our work together. We have each worked extensively with colleagues across the political aisle, and we understand the increased credibility that bipartisanship confers as well as the broader perspectives that result from including a range of expert voices. In addition, we need look no further than the 2020 election to understand that election protection is not a partisan issue. The threat came from a Republican president and Republicans who supported him. But Republicans and Democrats alike stood up, sometimes in the face of protests and threats, to do their jobs, speak the truth, and protect the integrity of our elections. They put country over party, and they deserve the gratitude and support of the American people, regardless of their ideologies on other issues. At States United, we believe strongly in an American consensus that transcends our differences, in the form of a commitment to shared principles of election integrity and protecting the will of the American voters. We will continue to rely and build on that consensus.

Third, while our work in the states is critical, the preservation of democracy requires a broader undertaking. It will depend on the continued dedication of many others and on bringing new allies into the fold. Greater investment in civic education, increased voter participation, and the restoration of a culture of trust in our elections are all pillars of a success-ful defense of democracy. We are thankful that States United is part of a constellation of organizations that have taken up this cause, including those that laid the groundwork for our successful efforts today. Many other committed nonprofit groups are at work safeguarding and expanding voting rights and access, providing legal and communications support, and building public engagement. Protecting our democracy is an all-hands-on-deck effort.

Fourth, there is a meaningful role for every person inter-ested in protecting free and fair elections. Community leaders and businesses can use their platforms to promote truthful information and refuse to amplify lies. They can publicly thank election officials, recognizing their dedication and promoting respect for these officials and the work that they do. They can use their platforms to praise bipartisan courage. Businesses specifically should recognize that free markets depend on democratic stability. Business leaders can speak out in support of valid election results and withhold donations from candidates who undermine them. They can also work to support democracy-strengthening legislation.[154]

If you are a member of the general public, there is plenty that you can do, too:

- Educate yourself. Resources detailing antidemocracy efforts are available on our website, as are reports refut-ing antidemocracy disinformation and providing accurate, straightforward election information (https://state-suniteddemocracy.org/resources/).

- Pay attention to antidemocracy efforts, learn to recognize them early, and call them out.
- Limit the spread of false information on social media by refusing to promote it or share it with others. Share truthful election information on your social networks.
- Vote in every election, not just in November every two or four years. Find out when your state holds primary elections and vote in those primaries. The primaries are where antidemocracy candidates can be stopped before they ever advance to November. Similarly, participate in your local elections. Antidemocracy candidates are running at the city, town, and county level, too.
- Support democracy by getting involved. Volunteer to be a poll worker at your local precinct or run for a state or local election position.
- Stay engaged, and encourage others.

The Antidemocracy Movement Is Growing More Sophisticated, but So Are We

The push to overturn the result of the last presidential election was preceded by months of disinformation, including from the sitting president himself. But most of the action—a crush of baseless lawsuits, pressure campaigns against state officials, schemes to prevent valid slates of electors from being counted, and, ultimately, the violence of January 6—took place over roughly nine weeks. The antidemocracy movement has had many months since then to study its mistakes and to plot a course forward.

What began as a campaign to overturn election results in swing states has metastasized into an intricate and nationwide movement. As we outlined in chapter 3, legislatures across the country are enacting or considering bills that would politicize, criminalize, or otherwise interfere with the administration of elections. At the same time, candidates across the country are running for statewide office on a platform of denying the results of the last election. At this writing, election deniers have already had some primary success, most prominently Douglas Mastriano of Pennsylvania, who secured his party's nomination for governor.[155] It is difficult to overstate the danger here: the refusal to certify the valid results of even one closely contested state in the next presidential election could cause untold chaos.

The gravity of the threat explains the breadth of our response. At States United we are working to protect elections, prevent political violence, promote truth in elections, and hold accountable those who step outside the bounds of our democracy. We understand the antidemocracy playbook, and we have effective responses across our areas of focus. We are in contact with state and local officials across the country, learning about their pressing concerns, and bolstering their defenses. Elections in this country may be changed forever; the array of antidemocracy efforts we have already seen are not going away. But neither are we. At States United, we are committed to this work and to growing our expertise and impact. We are resolved to protect free and fair elections in 2022, 2024, and beyond.

In the fight to protect our democracy, each of these efforts is vital. Every person who values free and fair elections has a role to play. Saving our democracy is everyone's job, and if we work together, relying on what we have learned already, we are well equipped to succeed.

Figure 5.   Election Day 2020 in South Carolina. Michael Ciaglo/ Getty Images News via Getty Images.

Conclusion

E ach election cycle, Americans generally have cast their votes and trusted the results. Close contests went to a recount or to the courts (occasionally both, as in 2000), but, in the end, elections had winners and losers. The results were respected. Democracy lumbered along—for most people, more a habit than a cause unto itself.

Then came 2020. A pandemic struck, and states were forced to adapt. Protesters surged to ballot-counting sites. State officials and election administrators who were accustomed to working in relative obscurity suddenly became the targets of a fusillade of lawsuits and a fog machine of disinformation. In some cases, their lives were threatened. The president of the United States personally pressured state legislators and state executives to throw out or falsify results. He leaned on his own vice president to claim an authority that did not exist and throw the final electoral count into chaos.

At the Capitol, a day of havoc and violence ended the American tradition of peaceful transfers of power.

The forces opposed to democracy in this country probed for weaknesses in our electoral system and attacked them with a relentless vigor, but the system held. We can take heart in that outcome. But we must learn from it, too. Democracy did not survive in 2020 by luck or by accident. It was saved by the courage of state officials—public servants who, in the face of unimaginable pressure, followed the law and honored the will of the people. If there is one overriding lesson from this tumultuous election, it is that these state officials form the backbone of our democracy. We owe them our gratitude. More than that, we owe them our support. That is why States United exists.

The antidemocracy movement in the United States is undaunted by its ultimate failure in 2020. If anything, it is treating the last election as a dry run—sharpening its tactics, probing for new weaknesses in our democratic machinery. The movement seeks the power and the pretext to simply toss out the results of a future election. That is the opposite of democracy, and a successful attempt would deliver a fatal blow to the American system.

The stakes of failure are no less than existential. But we do not believe American democracy will fail—not as long as we work to preserve and protect it. The last election nearly caused a breakdown of our electoral system, but it left us with an abiding vigilance. It taught us that we must push back against efforts in state legislatures to interfere with, and even criminalize, the routine administration of elections. It taught us that we must insist that our political candidates believe in the truth and respect the will of the voters. It taught us that any solution to our democratic crisis must be bipartisan: after all, Democrats and Republicans alike did their jobs faithfully in the last election, and the Republicans did so in defiance of a president from their own party who wanted them to neglect their duty to the voters. The last election also taught us that organizations like ours must be prepared to provide backup to the state officials who run, oversee, and defend our elections.

Responding to these needs is no small task. But we can be encouraged that this is the outcome Americans want. Voters indicate that denying the results of the last election is one of the least desirable qualities a political candidate can have.[156] They also believe, by an overwhelming majority, that counting every legal vote is more important than having their candidate win.[157] That is the essence of democracy.

The three of us joined forces in the summer of 2020 because we saw danger ahead for our country and believed we could help protect free and fair elections. When that danger came, thanks to heroic work in the states by public servants of both parties, democracy survived and endured. But we can no longer take that democracy for granted.

Preserving our electoral system, in the face of a determined movement that seeks to dismantle it, will require ongoing public engagement. That, too, is the essence of democracy. It is why we remain committed to this fight, and why we have hope for the future.

Acknowledgments

Although the three coauthors often write together, this publication is by far the most extensive we have ever jointly undertaken. It would not have been possible without the help of a great many people. Erin McClam and Amy Remus Scott spent countless hours coordinating the work of the authors, negotiating their different views, sharpening the arguments, refining the text, and otherwise acting as thought partners in every way. They are wonderful!

The authors would also like to thank the McCourtney Institute for Democracy at Penn State and its managing director, Christopher Beem, for the honor of being asked to produce this work and for their guidance. Gratitude also goes to Sarah Cypher, our editor, for her work on the various drafts and for her sage counsel throughout. We also want to thank Cornell University Press, in particular Bethany Wasik.

The authors express their profound gratitude to the States United family for their work on this publication—and on everything we do. In particular we want to recognize Fiona Dwyer-McNulty, Hank Sparks, and Lauren Meadows. We also are grateful to States United's generous supporters, board of directors, and advisory board, who have kept us on the path of bipartisan democracy defense from the start.

Last, but certainly not least, we want to thank our children and grandchildren, who remind us every day why this democracy is worth fighting for.

Notes

1 Melissa Quinn, "'Stand Back and Stand By': Trump Declines to Condemn White Supremacists at Debate," *CBS News*, September 30, 2020, https://www.cbsnews.com/news/proud-boys-stand-back-and-stand-by-trump-refuses-to-condemn-white-supremacists/.

2 Daniella Silva, "Trump's Call for Supporters to Watch Polls 'Very Carefully' Raises Concerns of Voter Intimidation," *NBC News*, September 30, 2020, https://www.nbcnews.com/news/us-news/trump-s-call-supporters-watch-polls-very-carefully-raises-concerns-n1241613.

3 Caitlin Dickson, "'Alarming Finding': 30 Percent of Republicans Say Violence May Be Needed to Save US, Poll Shows," *Yahoo! News*, October 31, 2021, https://news.yahoo.com/prri-poll-republicans-violence-040144322.html.

4 Annika Silva Leander et al., *The Global State of Democracy 2021: Building Resilience in a Pandemic Era* (Stockholm: International Institute for Democracy and Electoral Assistance, 2021), https://www.idea.int/gsod/sites/default/files/2021-11/the-global-state-of-democracy-2021_1.pdf.

5 Leander et al., *The Global State of Democracy*, iii.

6 The States United Democracy Center, Protect Democracy, and Law Forward, *A Democracy Crisis in the Making: How State Legislatures Are Politicizing, Criminalizing, and Interfering with Election Administration*, May 2022, 5, https://statesuniteddemocracy. org/wp-content/uploads/2022/05/DCITM_2022.pdf.

7 Justin Levitt, *The Truth about Voter Fraud* (New York: The Brennan Center for Justice, 2007): 5, https://www.brennancenter.org/ our-work/research-reports/truth-about-voter-fraud.

8 Levitt, *The Truth about Voter Fraud*, 5.

9 Levitt, 5.

10 Donald J. Trump (@realDonaldTrump), "This election is a total sham and a travesty. We are not a democracy!" Trump Twitter Archive, November 6, 2012, 11:33 PM EST, https://www. thetrumparchive.com/?searchbox=%22total+sham%22.

11 Donald J. Trump (@realDonaldTrump), "More reports of voting machines switching Romney votes to Obama. Pay close attention to the machines, don't let your vote be stolen," Trump Twitter Archive, November 6, 2012, 2:56 PM EST, https://www. thetrumparchive.com/?results=1&searchbox=%22more+ reports+of+voting+machines%22.

12 Donald J. Trump (@realDonaldTrump), "Crazy - Election officials saying . . ., " Trump Twitter Archive, October 31, 2014, 4:43 PM EST), https://www.thetrumparchive.com/?results= 1&searchbox=%22nothing+stopping+illegal+immigrants+ from+voting%22.

13 Donald J. Trump (@realDonaldTrump), "The election is absolutely being rigged . . ., " Trump Twitter Archive, October 16, 2016, 1:01 PM EST, https://www.thetrumparchive. com/?results=1&searchbox=%22election+is+absolutely+ being+%22.

14 "2016 Presidential Election Results," *New York Times*, last modified August 9, 2017, https://www.nytimes.com/elections/2016/results/president; Terrance Smith, "Trump Has Longstanding History of Calling Elections 'Rigged' If He Doesn't Like the Results," *ABC News,* November 11, 2020, https://abcnews.go.com/Politics/trump-longstanding-history-calling-elections-rigged-doesnt-results/story?id=74126926; Donald J. Trump (@realDonaldTrump), "In addition to winning the Electoral College in a landslide, I won the popular vote if you deduct the millions of people who voted illegally," Trump Twitter Archive, November 27, 2016, 3:30 PM EST, https://www.thetrumparchive.com/?results=1&searchbox=%22in+addition+to+winning+the+%22.

15 Steven Levitsky and Daniel Ziblatt, "The Crisis of American Democracy," *American Educator* 44, no. 3 (Fall 2020): 6–13, https://files.eric.ed.gov/fulltext/EJ1272137.pdf; Nicolas Berlinksi et al., "The Effects of Unsubstantiated Claims of Voter Fraud on Confidence in Elections," *Journal of Experimental Political Science* (2021): 1–16, https://cpb-us-e1.wpmucdn.com/sites.dartmouth.edu/dist/5/2293/files/2021/03/voter-fraud.pdf?_sm_au_=iHV4TH4F6TNDzFH7FcVTvKQkcK8MG.

16 Steve Coll, "Donald Trump's 'Fake News' Tactics," *The New Yorker,* December 3, 2017, https://www.newyorker.com/magazine/2017/12/11/donald-trumps-fake-news-tactics.

17 Natalie M. Scala et al., "Evaluating Mail-Based Security for Electoral Processes Using Attack Trees," *Risk Analysis: An International Journal,* published online ahead of print, January 24, 2022, https://onlinelibrary.wiley.com/doi/full/10.1111/risa.13876; Matthew Harwood, "Why a Vote-by-Mail Option Is Necessary, *Brennan Center for Justice,* last modified April 16, 2020, https://www.brennancenter.org/our-work/research-reports/why-vote-mail-option-necessary; Darrell M. West, "How Does Vote-By-Mail Work

and Does It Increase Election Fraud?" *Brookings Institution*, June 22, 2020, https://www.brookings.edu/policy2020/votervital/how-does-vote-by-mail-work-and-does-it-increase-election-fraud/.

18 Maryalice Parks and Kendall Karson, "A Step-By-Step Look at Trump's Falsehoods On Mail-In Voting: Analysis," *ABC News*, October 1, 2020, https://abcnews.go.com/Politics/step-step-trumps-falsehoods-mail-voting-analysis/story?id=73354979; Edward B. Foley, "A Big Blue Shift: Measuring an Asymmetrically Increasing Margin of Litigation," *Journal of Law and Politics* 28, no. 417 (2013): 501–46, http://www.lawandpolitics.org/hifi/files/content/vol-xxvii-no-4/Foley_Color_116.pdf; Richard L. Hasen, "Beyond the Margin of Litigation: Reforming US Election Administration to Avoid Electoral Meltdown," *Washington and Lee Law Review* 62, no. 3 (2005): 937–99, https://law2.wlu.edu/deptimages/Law%20Review/62-3 Hasen.pdf. See also David A. Graham, "The 'Blue Shift' Will Decide the Election," *The Atlantic*, last modified November 3, 2020, https://www.theatlantic.com/ideas/archive/2020/08/brace-blue-shift/615097/.

19 Donald J. Trump (@realDonaldTrump), "The United States cannot have all Mail In Ballots. It will be the greatest Rigged Election in history. People grab them from mailboxes, print thousands of forgeries and 'force' people to sign. Also, forge names. Some absentee OK, when necessary. Trying to use Covid for this Scam!" Trump Twitter Archive, May 24, 2020, 10:08 AM EST, https://www.thetrumparchive.com/?searchbox= %22thousands+of+forgeries%22.

20 Sam Levine, "Trump Attacks Mail-In Voting with New Series of False Claims," *The Guardian*, June 22, 2020, https://www.theguardian.com/us-news/2020/jun/22/trump-mail-in-voting-fraud-claims.

21 Donald J. Trump (@realDonaldTrump), "With Universal Mail-In Voting. . .," Trump Twitter Archive,

July 30, 2020, 8:46 AM EST, https://www.thetrumparchive. com/?searchbox=%222020+will+be+the+most%22.

22 "Transcript: 'Fox News Sunday' Interview with President Trump," *Fox News*, July 19, 2020, https://www.foxnews.com/politics/ transcript-fox-news-sunday-interview-with-president-trump/.

23 Louis Jacobson and Amy Sherman, "Donald Trump Says Joe Biden Can Only Win by a 'Rigged Election.' That's Wrong in Several Ways," *PolitiFact*, August 24, 2020, https://www.politifact.com/ factchecks/2020/aug/24/donald-trump/donald-trump-says-joe- biden-can-only-win-rigged-el/.

24 Channel News Asia, "Trump Declares Victory Prematurely, Says Will Go to Supreme Court to Dispute Election Count," November 4, 2020, Washington, DC, video, 9:45, https://www.youtube.com/ watch?v=NsI3jcgiIhA.

25 Channel News Asia, "Trump Declares . . ."

26 Al Schmidt (@Commish_Schmidt), "Philadelphia will NOT stop counting . . .," Twitter, November 4, 2020, 3:04 AM EST, https://twitter.com/commish_schmidt/status/1323898927666659328.

27 Jim Rutenberg et al., "77 Days: Trump's Campaign to Subvert the Election," *New York Times*, last modified June 15, 2021, https:// www.nytimes.com/2021/01/31/us/trump-election-lie.html.

28 James Verini, "He Wanted to Count Every Vote in Philadelphia. His Party Had Other Ideas," *New York Times,* last modified January 16, 2021, https://www.nytimes.com/2020/12/16/magazine/ trump-election-philadelphia-republican.html.

29 Ryan Suppe and Tommy Simmons, "Trump Supporters Gather for 'Stop the Steal' Rally in Boise," *Idaho Press,* November 7, 2020, https://www.idahopress.com/news/local/trump-supporters-gather- for-stop-the-steal-rally-in-boise/article_2110cb2a-35c6-52ba-a753- 336ad7b8bef3.html; Amber Jo Cooper, Kate Singh, and Courtney Fromm, "Trump Supporters Gather for 'Stop the Steal' Rally in

Colorado Springs," *Fox 21 News*, November 7, 2020, https://www.fox21news.com/top-stories/trump-supporters-gather-for-stop-the-steal-rally-in-colorado-springs/; Madeline Montgomery, "'Stop the Steal' Protestors Rally in Delray Beach to Show Support for Trump," *CBS 12 News*, November 7, 2020, https://cbs12.com/news/local/stop-the-steal-protestors-rally-in-delray-beach-to-show-support-for-trump.

30 Suppe and Simmons; Cooper, Singh, and Fromm; Montgomery.

31 "RELEASE: Members of the Voter Protection Program Bipartisan Advisory Board Issue Statement on Importance of Counting All Legally Cast Votes," *States United Democracy Center*, November 4, 2020, https://statesuniteddemocracy.org/2020/11/04/release-members-of-the-voter-protection-program-bipartisan-advisory-board-issue-statement-on-importance-of-counting-all-legally-cast-votes/.

32 Voter Protection Program et al., *What Police Need to Know about Protecting the Count*, accessed May 26, 2022, https://statesuniteddemocracy.org/wp-content/uploads/2020/11/Protecting-the-Count-Law-Enforcement-Guidance-11.4.20-FINAL.pdf.

33 "Rudy Giuliani Trump Campaign Philadelphia Press Conference at Four Seasons Total Landscaping," *Rev Transcriptions*, November 7, 2020, *Rudy Giuliani Trump Campaign Philadelphia Press Conference at Four Seasons Total Landscaping*, Rev Transcripts (Nov. 7, 2020), https://www.rev.com/blog/transcripts/rudy-giuliani-trump-campaign-philadelphia-press-conference-november-7.

34 Davey Alba, "'Release the Kraken,' a Catchphrase for Unfounded Conspiracy Theory, Trends on Twitter," *New York Times*, November 17, 2020, https://www.nytimes.com/2020/11/17/technology/release-the-kraken-a-catchphrase-for-unfounded-conspiracy-theory-trends-on-twitter.html.

35 Kelsey Vlamis, "Sidney Powell's 'Kraken' Lawsuits Failed Again, as Judges in Michigan, Georgia, Arizona, and Wisconsin Have

Now Dismissed Her Cases," *Business Insider*, December 10, 2020, https://www.businessinsider.com/sidney-powell-lawsuits-dismissed-michigan-georgia-arizona-wisconsin-2020-12; Kyle Cheney and Josh Gerstein, "Federal Judges Reject GOP Effort to Overturn Swing State Election Results," *Politico,* December 7, 2020, https://www.politico.com/news/2020/12/07/judge-rejects-overturn-michigan-election-results-443411.

36 *King et al. v. Whitmer et al.*, 20-cv-13134-LVP-RSW (E.D. Mich. 2020), ECF No. 62, at 35–36.

37 "Here's Every Word of the Second Jan. 6 Committee Hearing On Its Investigation," *NPR*, June 13, 2022, https://www.npr.org/2022/06/13/1104690690/heres-every-word-of-the-second-jan-6-committee-hearing-on-its-investigation.

38 "Here's Every Word . . ."

39 William Cummings, Joey Garrison, and Jim Sergent, "By the Numbers: President Donald Trump's Failed Efforts to Overturn the Election," *USA Today,* January 6, 2021, https://www.usatoday.com/in-depth/news/politics/elections/2021/01/06/trumps-failed-efforts-overturn-election-numbers/4130307001/; Russell Wheeler, "Trump's Judicial Campaign to Upend the 2020 Election: A Failure, but Not a Wipe-Out," *Brookings Institution*, November 30, 2021, https://www.brookings.edu/blog/fixgov/2021/11/30/trumps-judicial-campaign-to-upend-the-2020-election-a-failure-but-not-a-wipe-out/.

40 *Ward v. Jackson*, CV2020-015285 (Ariz. Super. Ct. Dec. 4, 2020), at 8; Maria Polletta, "Judge Rejects Arizona Republican Party's Attempt to Overturn Election Results; GOP Vows Appeal," *Arizona Republic,* December 4, 2020, https://www.azcentral.com/story/news/politics/elections/2020/12/04/arizona-judge-rejects-republican-effort-overturn-state-election-results/3821578001/.

41 *Ward v. Jackson*, CV-20-0343-AP/EL (Ariz. Sup. Ct. Dec. 8, 2020), at 6; *Ward v. Jackson, et al.*, 20-809 (U.S. Feb. 22, 2021),

denying petition for review; Maria Polletta, "Election Lawsuit from Arizona GOP Chair Kelli Ward Denied Hearing by US Supreme Court," *Arizona Republic*, February 22, 2021, https://www.azcentral.com/story/news/politics/elections/2021/02/22/us-supreme-court-wont-hear-kelli-wards-lawsuit-arizona-election/4544983001/.

42 *Wisconsin Voters Alliance v. Pence, et al.*, 1:20-cv-03791-JEB (D.D.C. Dec. 22, 2020), ECF No. 1.

43 *Wisconsin Voters Alliance v. Pence, et al.*, ECF No. 23.

44 *King et al. v. Whitmer et al.*, 20-cv-13134-LVP-RSW (E.D. Mich. 2020), ECF No. 172, at 1.

45 *O'Rourke et al. v. Dominion Voting Systems et al.*, 1:20-cv-03747-NRN (D. Colo. Aug. 3, 2021), ECF No. 136, at 5.

46 Cybersecurity and Infrastructure Security Agency, "Joint Statement from Elections Infrastructure Government Coordinating Council & The Election Infrastructure Sector Coordinating Executive Committees," November 12, 2020, https://www.cisa.gov/news/2020/11/12/joint-statement-elections-infrastructure-government-coordinating-council-election.

47 Bob Woodward and Robert Costa, *Peril* (New York: Simon & Schuster, 2021), 170.

48 Michael Balsamo, "Disputing Trump, Barr Says No Widespread Election Fraud," *Associated Press*, December 1, 2020, https://apnews.com/article/barr-no-widespread-election-fraud-b1f1488796c9a98c4b1a9061a6c7f49d.

49 Devan Cole, "Maricopa County Supervisor on Rejecting Calls from Trump Allies: 'Whatever Needed to Be Said, Needed to Be Said in a Courtroom,'" *CNN*, July 5, 2021, https://www.cnn.com/2021/07/05/politics/clint-hickman-trump-giuliani-election-calls-maricopa-county-cnntv/index.html.

50 Jess Bigood, "Aaron Van Langevelde's Speech about the 2020 Election: 'We Were Asked to Take Power We Didn't Have,'" *Boston*

Globe, July 5, 2021, https://www.bostonglobe.com/2021/07/05/
nation/aaron-van-langeveldes-speech-about-2020-election-we-were-
asked-take-power-we-didnt-have/.

51 Annie Grayer, Caroline Kelly, and Maegan Vazquez, "Michigan
Lawmakers Who Met with Trump Say They See Nothing to Change
Election Outcome," *CNN*, November 21, 2020, https://www.cnn.
com/2020/11/20/politics/michigan-house-speaker-will-meet-trump/
index.html.

52 William Bender and Angela Couloumbis, "President Trump
Invited Pa. Lawmakers to the White House. Then Everyone Went
Silent," *President Trump Invited Pa. Lawmakers to the White House.
Then Everyone Went Silent, Spotlight PA*, November 27, 2020, https://
www.pennlive.com/news/2020/11/president-trump-invited-pa-
lawmakers-to-the-white-house-then-everyone-went-silent.html.

53 Ryan Randazzo and Maria Polletta, "Arizona GOP Lawmakers
Hold Meeting on Election Outcome with Trump Lawyer Rudy
Giuliani," *Arizona Republic*, November 30, 2020, https://www.
azcentral.com/story/news/politics/elections/2020/11/30/republican-
lawmakers-arizona-hold-meeting-rudy-giuliani/6468171002;
States United Democracy Center, *Re: Request for Investigation
of John C. Eastman, California Bar Number 193726*, October 4,
2021, 13–14, https://statesuniteddemocracy.org/wp-content/
uploads/2021/10/10.4.21-FINAL-Eastman-Cover-Letter-
Memorandum.pdf; Alison Durkee, "Here's How the Trump
Campaign Is Still Trying to Overturn Biden's Victory," *Forbes,*
December 1, 2020, https://www.forbes.com/sites/alisondurkee/
2020/12/01/heres-how-the-trump-campaign-is-still-trying-to-
overturn-bidens-victory/?sh=1f6d91a43561.

54 "Transcript: President Trump's Phone Call with Georgia
Election Officials," *New York Times*, last modified January 5,
2021, https://www.nytimes.com/2021/01/03/us/politics/trump-
raffensperger-georgia-call-transcript.html.

55 "Michigan Law Is Clear: The Board of State Canvassers Must Immediately Certify the Vote," *States United Democracy Center*, November 22, 2020, https://statesuniteddemocracy.org/2020/11/22/michigan-law-is-clear-the-board-of-state-canvassers-must-immediately-certify-the-vote/.

56 Voter Protection Program, *VPP Backgrounder: Potential Criminal Issues Presented by Trump's Call to Raffensperger*, accessed May 26, 2022, https://statesuniteddemocracy.org/wp-content/uploads/2021/01/VPP-Backgrounder_Call-to-Raffensperger_-1.5.21-_FINAL.pdf.

57 Richard Fausset, "Georgia Jury to Consider Whether Trump Illegally Interfered in 2020 Election," *New York Times*, May 2, 2022, https://www.nytimes.com/2022/05/02/us/trump-election-georgia-grand-jury.html.

58 Farnoush Amiri, "EXPLAINER: How Fake Electors Tried to Throw Result to Trump," *Associated Press*, February 21, 2022, https://apnews.com/article/capitol-siege-joe-biden-presidential-elections-election-2020-electoral-college-311f88768b65f7196f52a4757dc162e4.

59 Marshall Cohen, Zachary Cohen, and Dan Merica, "Trump Campaign Officials, Led by Rudy Giuliani, Oversaw Fake Electors Plot in 7 States," *CNN*, January 20, 2022, https://www.cnn.com/2022/01/20/politics/trump-campaign-officials-rudy-giuliani-fake-electors/index.html.

60 Michael S. Schmidt, "Trump Says Pence Can Overturn His Loss in Congress. That's Not How It Works," *New York Times*, last modified April 30, 2021, https://www.nytimes.com/2021/01/05/us/politics/pence-trump-election.html. The limited role of the vice president in the certification of the electoral results was even reflected in testimony from Mr. Eastman himself following the 2000 presidential election. He stated then that under the Electoral Count Act, Congress "counts" the votes and is "the ultimate judge"

of disputes about the count and, in doing so, "is answerable to no one, not the Supreme Court of the United States, not the Supreme Court of Florida, in that judging," because that power is delegated to it by the Constitution. See also Florida State Legislature Select Joint Committee on the Manner of Appointment of Presidential Electors, "Manner and Appointment of Presidential Electors," November 29, 2000, Florida, video, 4:36:18, C-SPAN, https://www.c-span.org/video/?160847-1/manner-appointment-presidential-electors#.

61 Joshua Matz, Norman Eisen, and Harmann Singh, *Guide to Counting Electoral College Votes and the January 6, 2021, Meeting of Congress* (Voter Protection Program, 2021), https://statesuniteddemocracy.org/wp-content/uploads/2021/01/VPP-Guide-to-Counting-Electoral-Votes.pdf.

62 Donald J. Trump (@realDonaldTrump), "If Vice President @Mike_Pence comes through for us, we will win the Presidency . . .," " Trump Twitter Archive, January 6, 2021, 1:00 AM EST, https://www.thetrumparchive.com/?searchbox=%22mike+can+send+it%22.

63 Peter Baker, Maggie Haberman, and Annie Karni, "Pence Reached His Limit with Trump. It Wasn't Pretty," *New York Times*, January 12, 2021, https://www.nytimes.com/2021/01/12/us/politics/mike-pence-trump.html.

64 "Transcript of Trump's Speech at Rally before US Capitol Riot," *Associated Press*, January 13, 2021, https://apnews.com/article/election-2020-joe-biden-donald-trump-capitol-siege-media-e79eb51 64613d6718e9f4502eb471f27.

65 *Eastman v. Thompson et al.*, 8:22-cv-00099-DOC-DFM (C.D. Cal. Mar. 28, 2022), ECF. No. 260.

66 *Eastman v. Thompson et al.*, ECF No. 260, at 44.

67 Brittany Shepherd, "Pence, Defending His Actions on Jan. 6, Rebukes Trump as 'Wrong,'" *ABC News*, February 4, 2022, https://abcnews.go.com/Politics/pence-defending-actions-jan-rebukes-trump-wrong/story?id=82679131.

68 Shepherd, "Pence, Defending His Actions . . ."

69 Gabby Deutch and Kendrick McDonald, "The Top Election Myths Spreading Online and the Red-Rated Websites Promoting Them: 166 and Counting," NewsGuard, Jan. 20, 2021, https://www.newsguardtech.com/special-reports/election-misinformation-tracker/.

70 Deutch and McDonald, "The Top Election Myths . . ."

71 Christina Zhao, "Michael Flynn Says Trump Will Remain President in First Public Remarks since Pardon," *Newsweek*, December 12, 2020, https://www.newsweek.com/michael-flynn-says-trump-will-remain-president-first-public-remarks-since-pardon-1554374; see also Celine Castronuovo, "Flynn Delivers First Public Remarks since Trump Pardon at DC Rallies," *The Hill*, December 12, 2020, https://thehill.com/homenews/administration/529956-flynn-delivers-first-public-remarks-since-trump-pardon-at-dc-rallies/.

72 "US Election: Pro-Trump Rallies See Scuffles in US Cities," *BBC News*, December 13, 2020, https://www.bbc.com/news/election-us-2020-55292610; Shayan Sardarizadeh and Jessica Lussenhop, "The 65 Days That Led to Chaos at the Capitol," BBC News, January 10, 2021, https://www.bbc.co.uk/news/world-us-canada-55592332.

73 Aila Slisco, "Pro-Trump Martial-Law-Pushing Amanda Chase 'Getting Things in Order' to Run for Congress," *Newsweek*, November 8, 2021, https://www.newsweek.com/pro-trump-martial-law-pushing-amanda-chase-getting-things-order-run-congress-1647184.

74 Michael Ruiz, "Virginia Gubernatorial Candidate Says 'Trump Should Declare Martial Law,'" *Fox News*, December 17, 2020, https://www.foxnews.com/politics/virginia-amanda-chase-trump-martial-law.

75 "Business Entity Records—Stop the Steal, LLC," *Alabama Secretary of State,* accessed May 26, 2022, https://arc-sos.state.al.us/cgi/corpdetail.mbr/detail?corp=821150; Will Steakin, John Santucci, and Katherine Faulders, "Trump Allies Helped Plan, Promote Rally that Led to Capitol Attack," *ABC News,* January 8, 2021, https://abcnews.go.com/US/trump-allies-helped-plan-promote-rally-led-capitol/story?id=75119209.

76 Will Sommer, "'Stop the Steal' Organizer in Hiding after Denying Blame for Riot," *Daily Beast,* January 11, 2021, https://www.thedailybeast.com/stop-the-steal-organizer-in-hiding-after-denying-blame-for-riot; John Bowden, "Arizona GOP Asks If Followers Willing to Give Their Lives to 'Stop the Steal,'" *The Hill,* December 8, 2020, https://thehill.com/homenews/news/529195-arizona-gop-asks-if-followers-willing-to-give-their-life-to-stop-the-steal/.

77 "Rudy Giuliani Speech Transcript at Trump's Washington, D.C., Rally: Wants 'Trial by Combat,'" *Rev Transcriptions,* January 6, 2021, https://www.rev.com/blog/transcripts/rudy-giuliani-speech-transcript-at-trumps-washington-d-c-rally-wants-trial-by-combat.

78 Brian Naylor, "Read Trump's Jan. 6 Speech, a Key Part of Impeachment Trial," *NPR,* February 10, 2021, https://www.npr.org/2021/02/10/966396848/read-trumps-jan-6-speech-a-key-part-of-impeachment-trial.

79 Rory Carroll, "Baked Alaska, the QAnon Shaman . . . Who Led the Storming of the Capitol?" *The Guardian,* January 7, 2021, https://www.theguardian.com/us-news/2021/jan/07/baked-alaska-the-qanon-shaman-who-led-the-storming-of-the-capitol.

80 The States United Democracy Center, Protect Democracy, and Law Forward, *A Democracy Crisis in the Making: How State Legislatures Are Politicizing, Criminalizing, and Interfering with Election Administration,* April 2021, https://statesuniteddemocracy.

org/wp-content/uploads/2021/04/FINAL-Democracy-Crisis-Report-April-21.pdf.

81 See "State Voting Rights Tracker," *Voting Rights Lab*, accessed May 31, 2022, https://tracker.votingrightslab.org/.

82 Mark Niesse, "How Georgia's Voting Law Works," *Atlanta Journal-Constitution*, May 6, 2021, https://www.ajc.com/politics/how-georgias-new-voting-law-works/GF6PLR44PNESPKR5FXCBE7VEOY/.

83 H.B. 2492, 55th Leg., Reg. Sess. (Ariz. 2022).

84 Nick Corasaniti, "Arizona Passes Proof-Of-Citizenship Law for Voting in Presidential Elections," *New York Times*, March 31, 2022, https://www.nytimes.com/2022/03/31/us/politics/arizona-voting-bill-citizenship.html.

85 The States United Democracy Center, Protect Democracy, and Law Forward, *A Democracy Crisis in the Making: How State Legislatures are Politicizing, Criminalizing, and Interfering with Election Administration*, May 2022, 6, https://statesuniteddemocracy.org/wp-content/uploads/2021/04/FINAL-Democracy-Crisis-Report-April-21.pdf.

86 *A Democracy Crisis in the Making,* April 2021.

87 *A Democracy Crisis in the Making,* May 2022, 4.

88 S.B. 202, 2021–22 Reg. Sess. (Ga. 2021); *A Democracy Crisis in the Making,* April 2021, 12–15.

89 H.B. 2332, 2021–22 Reg. Sess. (Kan. 2021).

90 The States United Democracy Center, Protect Democracy, and Law Forward, *Democracy Crisis Report Update: New Data and Trends Show the Warning Signs Have Intensified in the Last Two Months*, June 10, 2021, 8, https://statesuniteddemocracy.org/wp-content/uploads/2021/06/Democracy-Crisis-Part-II_June-10_Final_v7.pdf.

91 Steve Peoples, Marc Levy, and Farnoush Amiri, "How Pa. GOP Pick Could Turn Election Lies into Action," *Associated Press*,

May 18, 2022, https://apnews.com/article/2022-midterm-elections-pennsylvania-donald-trump-presidential-biden-cabinet-2594fd3fe8 6b6fb53c5011a7f76c2353.

92 "Select Committee Demands Information on Efforts to Send False 'Alternate Electors' to Congress and Otherwise Interfere with Election Certification," *Press Releases: Select Committee to Investigate the January 6th Attack on the United States Capitol*, February 15, 2022, https://january6th.house.gov/news/press-releases/select-committee-demands-information-efforts-send-false-alternate-electors.

93 Craig Mauger, "DePerno Wins GOP Attorney General Race after Runoff; Karamo Wins SOS Endorsement," *The Detroit News*, April 23, 2022, https://www.detroitnews.com/story/news/politics/2022/04/23/michigan-gop-convention-test-trumps-influence-begins-grand-rapids/7365309001/.

94 "Endorsement of Mark Finchem," *Save America*, September 13, 2021, https://www.donaldjtrump.com/news/news-rbycqm3btr682.

95 Ed Pilkington, "'This Should Terrify the Nation': The Trump Ally Seeking to Run Arizona's Elections," *The Guardian*, February 21, 2022, https://www.theguardian.com/us-news/2022/feb/21/mark-finchem-trump-arizona-elections-secretary-of-state.

96 Russell Berman, "The Desperate Scramble to Stop an Insider Election Threat," *The Atlantic*, November 14, 2021, https://www.theatlantic.com/politics/archive/2021/11/pennsylvania-election-threat/620684/.

97 Berman, "The Desperate Scramble . . ."

98 Berman, "The Desperate Scramble . . ."

99 Berman, "The Desperate Scramble . . .;" Jeremy Herb, "How January 6 Changed What It Means to be a Republican in One Pennsylvania County," *CNN*, January 5, 2022, https://www.cnn.com/2022/01/05/politics/jan-6-capitol-riot-lancaster-republicans/index.html.

100 Herb, "How January 6 Changed What It Means . . ."

101 Charles Homans, "In Bid for Control of Elections, Trump Loyalists Face Few Obstacles," *New York Times*, last modified December 15, 2021, https://www.nytimes.com/2021/12/11/us/politics/trust-in-elections-trump-democracy.html.

102 "Secretary of State Races in 2022," *The States United Democracy Center*, last modified March 1, 2022, https://statesuniteddemocracy.org/wp-content/uploads/2022/03/sos_deniers-2.html#3_Secretary_of_State_Races_in_2022. See "Georgia" for one example.

103 Rachel Janfaza and Deanna Hackney, "Kemp Booed and Raffensperger Censured at Georgia GOP Convention," *CNN*, last modified June 5, 2021, https://www.cnn.com/2021/06/05/politics/brad-raffensperger-brian-kemp-georgia-republican-convention/index.html.

104 Jonathan J. Cooper, "Arizona Republicans Censure Cindy McCain, GOP governor," *Associated Press*, January 23, 2021, https://apnews.com/article/donald-trump-race-and-ethnicity-censures-arizona-lawsuits-a50165b9d5c4468d5d1bb434c5e9c80a; Kyung Lah, "Arizona GOP Censures Flake, Ducey, and McCain, Signaling a Fractured Party in a Key Swing State," *CNN Politics*, last modified January 24, 2021, https://www.cnn.com/2021/01/23/politics/arizona-gop-censure-mccain-flake-ducey/index.html.

105 Alana Wise, "RNC Votes to Censure Reps. Liz Cheney and Adam Kinzinger over Work with Jan. 6 Panel," *NPR*, February 4, 2022, https://www.npr.org/2022/02/04/1078316505/rnc-censure-liz-cheney-adam-kinzinger-jan-6-committee-capitol.

106 Wise, "RNC Votes to Censure Reps. . . . "

107 The Brennan Center for Justice and the Bipartisan Policy Center, *Election Officials under Attack: How to Protect Administrators and Safeguard Democracy*, June 16, 2021, 4, https://www.brennancenter.org/our-work/policy-solutions/election-officials-under-attack.

108 Linda So and Jason Szep, "US Election Workers Get Little Help from Law Enforcement as Terror Threats Mount," *Reuters*, September 8, 2021, https://www.reuters.com/investigates/special-report/usa-election-threats-law-enforcement/.

109 So and Szep, "US Election Workers Get Little Help . . ."

110 So and Szep, "US Election Workers Get Little Help . . ."

111 So and Szep, "US Election Workers Get Little Help . . ."

112 Michael Wines, "After a Nightmare Year, Election Officials Are Quitting," *New York Times*, July 2, 2021, https://www.nytimes.com/2021/07/02/us/politics/2020-election-voting-officials.html.

113 *A Democracy Crisis in the Making*, May 2022, 43–44.

114 Rosalind S. Helderman, Isaac Arnsdorf, and Josh Dawsey, "Doug Mastriano's Pa. Victory Could Give 2020 Denier Oversight of 2024," *Washington Post*, May 18, 2022, https://www.washingtonpost.com/politics/2022/05/18/doug-mastrianos-pa-victory-could-give-2020-denier-oversight-2024/.

115 "Seven in Ten Americans Say the Country Is in Crisis, at Risk of Failing," *Ipsos*, January 3, 2022, https://www.ipsos.com/en-us/seven-ten-americans-say-country-crisis-risk-failing.

116 SSRS, *Overview for CNN*, September 15, 2021, http://cdn.cnn.com/cnn/2021/images/09/15/rel5e.-.elections.pdf.

117 "Jurisdictions Previously Covered by Section 5," US Department of Justice, accessed June 7, 2022, https://www.justice.gov/crt/jurisdictions-previously-covered-section-5.

118 *Shelby County v. Holder*, 570 U.S. 529 (2013).

119 *Brnovich v. Democratic National Committee*, 594 U.S. ___ (2021).

120 "Fact Sheet: The John Lewis Voting Rights Advancement Act," *Brennan Center for Justice*, December 22, 2021, https://www.brennancenter.org/our-work/research-reports/john-lewis-voting-rights-advancement-act.

121 Wendy Weiser, Daniel Weiner, and Emil Mella Pablo, "Breaking Down the Freedom to Vote Act," *Brennan Center for Justice*, September 23, 2021, https://www.brennancenter.org/our-work/research-reports/breaking-down-freedom-vote-act.

122 "AZ GOP v. Hobbs—Early Voting and Elections Procedures Manual (AZ)," *States United Democracy Center*, accessed May 31, 2022, https://statesuniteddemocracy.org/legal/azgopvhobbs-legal/.

123 S.B. 1320, 40th Leg., 1st Reg. Sess. (Ariz. 1991).

124 *Arizona Republican Party v. Hobbs*, CV-22-0048-SA (Ariz. Sup. Ct., April 5, 2022), order declining jurisdiction.

125 *Arizona Republican Party v. Hobbs* (Ariz. Mohave Cty. Super. Ct., May 17, 2022), complaint.

126 Charles R. Davis, "Republicans Failed to End Mail-In Voting in Arizona. But Secretary of State Katie Hobbs Says They're 'Laying the Groundwork' to Steal the 2024 Election," *Business Insider*, June 6, 2022, https://www.businessinsider.com/arizona-judge-rules-against-republican-effort-ban-mail-in-voting-2022-6.

127 "Private Voter Information in Pennsylvania," *States United Democracy Center*, accessed May 31, 2022, https://statesuniteddemocracy.org/legal/pavoter-legal/.

128 "Pennsylvania State Officials Sue to Block State Senate Subpoena Seeking Private Voter Information," *States United Democracy Center*, September 23, 2021, https://statesuniteddemocracy.org/2021/09/23/pa-lawsuit/.

129 "LULAC v. Elfant," *States United Democracy Center*, accessed May 31, 2022, https://statesuniteddemocracy.org/legal/lulacelfant-legal/.

130 "LUPE v. Abbott," *States United Democracy Center*, accessed May 31, 2022, https://statesuniteddemocracy.org/legal/lupeabbot-legal/.

131 "Amicus Brief: Longoria v. Paxton—Vote by Mail (TX)," *States United Democracy Center*, accessed May 31, 2022, https://statesuniteddemocracy.org/legal/txvotebymail-legal/.

132 "Primary Update: States United Action Releases New Data on Election Deniers Running for Statewide Offices that Run, Oversee, and Protect Our Elections," *States United Democracy Center*, May 6, 2022, https://statesuniteddemocracy.org/2022/05/06/trackerreleaseupdate2/.

133 Barry C. Burden and Trey Grayson, *Report on the Cyber Ninjas Review of the 2020 Presidential and US Senatorial Elections in Maricopa County, Arizona* (States United Democracy Center, June 2021), https://statesuniteddemocracy.org/wp-content/uploads/2021/06/6.22.21-SUDC-Report-re-Cyber-Ninjas-Review-FINAL.pdf.

134 See Zach Montellaro, "Trump Audit Excitement Meets with Fear from Election Officials," *Politico*, June 30, 2021, https://www.politico.com/news/2021/06/30/2020-election-audit-arizona-497049; Charles R. Davis, "The Arizona Election 'Audit' Is a Partisan and Amateurish Endeavor that 'Should Not Be Trusted,' Expert Review Finds," *Business Insider*, June 22, 2021, https://www.businessinsider.com/arizona-election-audit-should-not-be-trusted-expert-review-finds-2021-6; Rosalind Helderman, "Ballots and Voting Equipment Are Moved Again as Review of 2020 Election Drags on in Arizona's Maricopa County," *Washington Post*, July 1, 2021, https://www.washingtonpost.com/politics/arizona-maricopa-county-audit-ballot-review/2021/07/01/3576eadc-d4f2-11eb-a53a-3b5450fdca7a_story.html; Jeremy Duda, "Fann Says Audit Team, Maricopa County Have Different Ballot Totals," *AZ Mirror*, July 13, 2021, https://www.azmirror.com/blog/fann-says-audit-team-maricopa-county-have-different-ballot-totals/; Joe Dana, "No, the Arizona Senate GOP's 'Audit' Did Not Find 57,000 Questionable Ballots," *12 News*, last modified November 12, 2021, https://www.12news.com/article/

news/verify/arizona-audit-57000-ballots-senate-gop/75-a0a98638-f74f-4861-b6e0-e1d53c3eec06.

135 Voter Protection Program et al., *Preparing for Election Day and Post-Election Demonstrations,* accessed May 31, 2022, https://statesuniteddemocracy.org/wp-content/uploads/2020/10/Preparing-for-Election-Day-and-Post-Election-Demonstrations-FINAL-10.31.20.pdf.

136 "Voter Intimidation Toolkit," *States United Democracy Center,* accessed May 31, 2022, https://statesuniteddemocracy.org/resources/voter-intimidation-toolkit/.

137 "Institute for Constitutional Advocacy and Protection," *Georgetown Law,* accessed May 31, 2022, https://www.law.georgetown.edu/icap/.

138 The States United Democracy Center and the Institute for Constitutional Advocacy and Protection, *Countering Bigotry and Extremism in the Ranks: A First Amendment Guide for Law Enforcement Agencies,* April 28, 2022, https://statesuniteddemocracy.org/wp-content/uploads/2022/04/2022.4.7.-Countering-Bigotry-and-Extremism-in-the-Ranks.pdf.

139 For a preview of our forthcoming report, see "Midterms 2022: The Poll Observer Landscape," *States United Democracy Center,* accessed May 31, 2022, https://statesuniteddemocracy.org/resources/midterm-pollobservers/.

140 *District of Columbia v. Proud Boys International, LLC et al.,* 1:21-cv-03267 (D.D.C. December 14, 2021), ECF No. 1.

141 "Amicus Brief: Donald J. Trump v. Bennie G. Thompson et al. (Executive Privilege Case)," *States United Democracy Center,* accessed May 31, 2022, https://statesuniteddemocracy.org/legal/trump-scotus-ep/.

142 Adam Liptak, "In Rebuke to Trump, Supreme Court Allows Release of Jan. 6 Files," *New York Times,* January 19, 2022, https://

www.nytimes.com/2022/01/19/us/politics/trump-supreme-court-jan-6.html.

143 This writing was completed before the House of Representatives' select committee finished its public hearings.

144 States United Democracy Center, *Re: Request for Investigation of John C. Eastman, California Bar Number 193726,* October 4, 2021, https://statesuniteddemocracy.org/wp-content/uploads/2021/10/10.4.21-FINAL-Eastman-Cover-Letter-Memorandum.pdf.

145 The Obama White House ethics adviser who signed the complaint was Norm Eisen, one of the authors of this book.

146 *Texas v. Pennsylvania et al.,* 22O155 (U.S. Sup. Ct. December 9, 2020), motion to intervene.

147 States United Democracy Center, *Re: Matter of John Eastman, Case Number 21-O-12451,* November 16, 2021, https://statesuniteddemocracy.org/wp-content/uploads/2021/11/Supplemental-Letter-to-State-Bar-of-California.pdf.

148 "State Bar Announces John Eastman Ethics Investigation," *The State Bar of California,* March 1, 2022, https://www.calbar.ca.gov/About-Us/News/News-Releases/state-bar-announces-john-eastman-ethics-investigation.

149 States United Democracy Center, *Re: Matter of John Eastman, Case Number 21-O-12451,* April 14, 2022, https://statesuniteddemocracy.org/wp-content/uploads/2022/04/04.14.22_Case-Number-21-O-12451_Second-Supplemental-Filing_Final1.pdf.

150 *Re: Matter of John Eastman . . .,* April 14, 2022, 3.

151 States United Democracy Center, *Re: Request for Investigation of Jenna L. Ellis (also known as Jenna Lynn Rives), Colorado Registration Number 44026,* May 4, 2022, https://statesuniteddemocracy.org/wp-content/uploads/2022/05/2022.05.04-Jenna-Ellis-complaint.pdf.

152 Philip Bump, "'2000 Mules' Offers the Least Convincing Election-Fraud Theory Yet," *Washington Post*, last modified May 17, 2022, https://www.washingtonpost.com/politics/2022/05/11/2000-mules-offers-least-convincing-election-fraud-theory-yet/.

153 Ali Swenson, "Fact Focus: Gaping Holes in the Claim of 2K Ballot 'Mules,'" Associated Press, May 3, 2022, https://apnews.com/article/2022-midterm-elections-covid-technology-health-arizona-e1b49d2311bf900f44fa5c6dac406762.

154 Rebecca Henderson, "Business Can't Take Democracy for Granted," *Harvard Business Review*, January 8, 2021, https://hbr.org/2021/01/business-cant-take-democracy-for-granted.

155 Other election deniers had not yet been nominated by voters at this writing but had been endorsed by their state Republican Party. As we discussed in chapter 3, Matthew DePerno, a candidate for Michigan attorney general, and Kristina Karamo, a candidate for Michigan secretary of state, are examples.

156 Chuck Todd et al., "The Most Popular—and Unpopular—2022 Candidate Qualities," *NBC News*, March 30, 2022, https://www.nbcnews.com/politics/meet-the-press/popular-unpopular-2022-candidate-qualities-rcna22151.

157 The Mellman Group, *Our Recent National Poll*, November 3, 2020, https://statesuniteddemocracy.org/wp-content/uploads/2020/11/20mem1103-f4-Voter-Protection.pdf

About the Authors

Joanna Lydgate is the cofounder and chief executive officer of the States United Democracy Center. Prior to launching States United, she served as the chief deputy attorney general of Massachusetts, where she spent several years leading the state's most prominent litigation, working with a bipartisan team of colleagues from across the country. Lydgate also oversaw criminal enforcement for the Attorney General's Office, coordinating daily with local, state, and federal law enforcement partners.

Norm Eisen is the cofounder and executive chair of the States United Democracy Center. An attorney and author who has served in a broad array of government roles, he was special counsel and special assistant to President Barack Obama for ethics and government reform from 2009 to 2011, and US ambassador to the Czech Republic from 2011 to 2014. Eisen served as special counsel to the House Judiciary Committee for the impeachment and trial of President Donald Trump from 2019 to 2020. His memoir of the impeachment is *A Case for the American People*. Eisen is the author or editor of three other books, the most recent of which is *Overcoming Trumpery: How to Restore Ethics, the Rule of Law, and Democracy*, published in March by Brookings Institution Press.

Christine Todd Whitman is the cofounder and cochair of the States United Democracy Center. She was governor of New Jersey from 1994 to 2001 and administrator of the Environmental Protection Agency under President George W. Bush from 2001 to 2003. Governor Whitman is cochair of the Meridian Institute Board and chair of the American Security Project. Previously she served as cochair of the Commission on the Rule of Law and Democracy at the Brennan Center at New York University. Additionally she is vice chair of the Eisenhower Fellowships Board of Trustees and cochair of the National Institute for Civil Discourse. She is the author of the *New York Times* bestseller *It's My Party Too: The Battle for the Heart of the GOP and the Future of America.*